The experts
praise for Ge
POWER T

Here's what the have to say:

"YOU HAVE A WINNER IN *POWER TALKING*. IT'S READABLE, SPRIGHTLY, POSITIVE, AND THE WAY TO POWER IS QUITE EVIDENT. THE INTEREST LEVEL IS HIGH."
—Norman Vincent Peale

"*POWER TALKING* WILL HAVE A POWERFUL, POSITIVE IMPACT ON THE LIVES OF ALL WHO READ IT . . . EVEN IF THEY ONLY TAKE ADVANTAGE OF ONE OF THE FIFTY IDEAS IN IT AND USE IT WELL."
—Tom Hopkins, author of *How to Master the Art of Selling*

"THE FIRST CHAPTER ALONE IS WORTH THE PRICE OF THE BOOK!"
—Stew Leonard, CEO and President, Stew Leonard's World's Largest Dairy Store

"YOU'LL SOAR TO NEW HEIGHTS OF EFFECTIVENESS WITH THIS INCREDIBLE TOOL."
—Scott de Garmo, Editor-in-Chief and Publisher, *Success* magazine

"GEORGE WALTHER HAS REALLY HIT A HOME RUN WITH HIS NEW BOOK . . . FILLED WITH PRACTICAL, EASY TO REMEMBER IDEAS FOR SPEAKING AND THINKING POSITIVELY."
—Toby Suhm, Director of Customer Satisfaction, US WEST New Vector

"EVERYONE SHOULD READ IT AND USE IT—IMMEDIATELY!"
—Brian Tracy, author of *The Psychology of Achievement*

Berkley Books by George R. Walther

PHONE POWER
POWER TALKING

POWER TALKING

50 WAYS TO SAY WHAT YOU MEAN AND GET WHAT YOU WANT

GEORGE R. WALTHER

BERKLEY BOOKS, NEW YORK

This Berkley book contains the complete text of the original hardcover edition. It has been completely reset in a typeface designed for easy reading, and was printed from new film.

POWER TALKING

A Berkley Book / published by arrangement with the author

PRINTING HISTORY
G.P. Putnam's Sons edition / May 1991
Published simultaneously in Canada
Berkley edition / June 1992

ISBN: 0-425-13328-1

A BERKLEY BOOK ® TM 757,375
Berkley Books are published by The Berkley Publishing Group,
200 Madison Avenue, New York, New York 10016.
The name "BERKLEY" and the "B" logo
are trademarks belonging to Berkley Publishing Corporation.

PRINTED IN THE UNITED STATES OF AMERICA

10 9 8 7 6 5 4 3

This book is dedicated to my daughter,
KELCIE PAIGE.

*You will hear the sound
of one man clapping.*

Acknowledgments

This book is the direct result of enthusiastic feedback from clients, readers, users of my audio and video tapes, and audience members who asked for more of the "Power Talking" concepts introduced in *Phone Power*. Thank you all for inspiring me to write *Power Talking*.

It's a long trail from concept to finished book. Adrienne Ingrum got me started by encouraging me to "put it in writing." My agents, Arthur and Richard Pine, handled the publishing negotiations and allowed me to concentrate on creating my best work. Laurie Larsen's nimble fingers and sharp eyes helped with much of the word processing. My Putnam editorial team, Rena Wolner and Christine Pepe, provided superb support, expertly pared the manuscript, and helped me polish my writing.

Many colleagues in the National Speakers Association have provided priceless fellowship and professional support. I appreciate their abundant suggestions and assistance.

No author could ask for a better "home team." Thank you, Julie, for your contributions of ideas and time. I respect and appreciate your rare and marvelous combination of raw brainpower and levelheadedness. And most important of all, thank you for being such a wonderful mother.

Contents

POWER TALKING

Introduction

Two employees, in adjacent offices, each tell their supervisors that they haven't completed their monthly status reports on time:

Employee A says:

"Well, John, to tell you the truth, there were so many distractions this week that, I hate to say it, but I just couldn't finish the report on time. It's not my fault, I couldn't help it. You know what I mean. I'm afraid I can't complete it until around the middle of next week."

Employee B says:

"John, my monthly status report is not yet finished. We can review my outline of the highlights together now, and I'll have the completed report for you before Thursday morning. I take responsibility for the delay. I decided that some other projects warranted a higher priority."

Which employee has better career prospects?

You and a friend own identical cars, and they both start making peculiar squealing sounds somewhere in the engine compartment. First thing Monday morning, each of you takes your car to a different nearby dealer.

Dealer A says:

"Gee, I don't know what to tell you. Our service department won't be open until about 9:00 or so. It's Monday, you know. I couldn't help you myself. I'm only in the used car sales department. You'll just have to check back a little later. Sorry."

Dealer B says:

"I'll be glad to help you. The service department will be open by 9:00. Meanwhile, I can help you fill out the Work Order form. That way you'll be all set when they open in a few minutes."

Which dealership is likely to create satisfied customers who recommend it to their friends?

You decide to computerize your home finances. You visit two software stores to find out which personal accounting program will work best for you.

Salesperson A says:

"The problem is, there are so many different programs, it's almost impossible to figure out which one's right for you. I'd hate to see you get stuck with the wrong one. Let's see now, which might be the best program for me to sell you?"

Salesperson B says:

"Our challenge is to find out which program will best match your needs, and I'll be happy to help you with that. I want to be sure that we select the software that you'll be happiest with. Let's talk about what you want the program to do, and then I'll recommend the best choice."

Which salesperson will probably win your business?

In each case, A conveyed the same basic information as B. Yet, you, as the supervisor, or car owner, or software shopper, experienced a very different reaction to what each person said.

The big distinctions lie in how A and B expressed themselves. They both used common language; each said about the same number of words; neither spoke more intelligently than the other. Yet, the impact of what each person communicated differed dramatically.

All day, every day, people size **you** up based on the way you talk. In these examples, B is clearly going to move ahead faster and experience more professional success, make customers happier, enjoy stronger friendships, and generate higher sales than A.

This book shows you how to ensure that you're always in the "B" position. The Power Talking techniques you'll learn here help you create consistently positive impressions whenever others hear you. They apply equally well at home with family and friends, or at work with customers, supervisors, and peers.

Power Talking shows you how to speak the language of success. Use the words and phrases you read here, and you will experience greater professional achievements, more harmonious relationships with friends and colleagues, a happier family life, better emotional and physical health, and yes, you'll even make more money.

Learning to speak more powerfully isn't like studying Latin or taking German classes. There's no vocabulary quiz. You already know all the words and phrases you'll ever need to know. It's how you put those everyday expressions together and how you use them that counts.

This book presents simple ways to put positive thinking theories to work in your life. You don't even need to finish reading this introduction before you start reaping the benefits.

I've gathered 50 specific expressions you can use to help make sure things go your way, and covered each one in its own chapter. You can begin with any of the 50, start at the beginning or at the end. Or just keep flipping through the book, adopting phrase after phrase. When you spot a powerless expression that you recognize as part of your present daily speaking habits, read that chapter. Maybe you'll notice a familiar phrase like "I'll try," or "that could be a problem," or "I'll be honest with you," and say to yourself, "Hey, I say that all the time. What's wrong with it? How is my use of that expression holding me back? What should I be saying instead?" Read that chapter immediately.

The 50 chapters are grouped into sections, each focusing on one of the traits shared by successful, happy people. Power Talkers, for instance, rebound resiliently from apparent setbacks. Section III, "Rebound Resiliently," includes several examples of get-back-on-track phrases you can use when things aren't going quite the way you'd like.

Every chapter deals with a specific, all-too-common phrase, and includes personal anecdotes and stories about encounters with clients, audience members, friends or family. Then, each of the 50 chapters proceeds with the rationale behind the substitution I've recommended.

And finally, each chapter concludes with a "Quick Reference: What You Can Do Right Now" summary. There, you'll find common power*less* phrases that you may be using habitually and unwittingly, along with their recommended Power Talking replacements.

So, let's start! Flip through the book right now. Find a powerless phrase that you know you sometimes use. Maybe it's "I'll have to . . ." Read Chapter 1 and decide to banish that phrase starting *now*. Purge it from your vocabulary. Today, begin substituting the phrase, "I'll be glad to . . ." and keep it up. Then, move ahead to another phrase that catches your interest. Don't worry about reading the chapters or sections "in order." Do read them all.

You're going to see immediate results. Creating long-term changes in your life by changing the way you speak isn't easy—and it's also not terribly difficult. Start with one phrase right now. Get those powerless phrases out of your vocabulary and start Power Talking.

POWER TALKERS . . .

I. Project Positive Expectations

The most noticeable characteristic of Power Talkers is that they project positive expectations, both for themselves and for others. You're probably familiar with the concepts of positive thinking as detailed in Dr. Norman Vincent Peale's classic, *The Power of Positive Thinking*. As he put it, "When you change your thoughts, you change your life." But you can't just sit in a corner and think positively—that won't change your life. You need to interact positively with others. I agree with Dr. Peale's advice about positive thinking, and recommend that you take one more step.

Power Talkers go beyond **thinking** positively—they **talk** positively, too. Notice the big difference between a person who says, "I can never remember anyone's name" vs. the person who says, "I'm working to improve my memory."

I recently had my home remodeled, and I noticed that the contractors who said, "I'll try and get back to you by tomorrow" rarely did. Those who said, "I will have an answer for you before 5:00 tomorrow" followed through and lived up to their commitments. That's because the expectations they set didn't just influence me, the listener. They influenced themselves as well. When you set positive expectations for others, you're setting them for yourself, too. Making a commitment increases your reliability in the other person's eyes, and it also helps you program yourself to follow through.

One manager of a public utility company in San Francisco noticed that her people often revealed their gloomy morale through their routine daily greetings. She'd overhear co-workers passing in the hallways greeting each other with, "Hey, how's it going?" The most common responses ran along the lines of, "Oh, OK, I guess," and "Only four more days 'til the weekend." She suspected that these comments brought everyone's attitude down.

During her next staff meeting, she explained her theory and implemented a reward system to encourage positive responses. She designated individuals to serve as "mystery greeters," so other employees wouldn't know when their responses were being assessed. The greeters asked co-workers how they were, and noted those who offered positive responses. Those who the "mystery greeters" felt contributed most to a positive atmosphere were recognized and rewarded with a small prize at the end of the day. The result?

"It made a huge difference almost overnight. Once people became aware of the effect their greetings and responses had on each other, I heard them saying things like: 'Great!' or 'I'm doing really well today, how 'bout you?' and so on. They all started believing each other, and really did feel much better. You could easily gauge the difference in morale."

In the following chapters you'll meet people who focus on affirmative language and action, who set optimistic expectations for themselves and others, and who think, speak, and behave positively. They use their own language to help create success for themselves. You can, too.

1. I'll Be Glad To!

Your co-worker went to lunch without arranging for phone coverage. You're working through lunch so you can go home a little early. Her phone, on the desk beside yours, rings and rings and rings. Annoyed, you finally decide to answer it.

Say out loud to yourself:

"I'll have to take a message and she won't get it for another hour or so."

Now, say:

"I'll be glad to take your message and make sure she gets it before 1:30."

Which will give the caller the more favorable impression? Which will make you feel better about taking the message?

"Good Evening, thank you for calling the GE Answer Center, I'm Miss Cooley, how may I help you?"

The GE Answer Center uses my Power Talking techniques for its employee training program. I like to call in anonymously from time to time and check to see how consistently the Center's employees apply their training.

When my wife and I had decided to buy a freezer, I called (anonymously, of course) the Answer Center late one Sunday night for product information before visiting a dealer. I started by asking about energy consumption:

"Which type of freezer is more energy efficient: upright or chest style?"

Miss Cooley didn't sound old enough to have purchased

many freezers herself, and I was a little skeptical about her firsthand knowledge.

> *"That's a good question. I'm in training now, and I'd like to compare the efficiency ratings of several models for you."*

She'd LIKE to? I'm used to people saying something more along the lines of,

> "Well, I'm still only a trainee, so I couldn't tell you for sure. What I'd have to do is look up some different models and see if I can figure that out."

Rather than making it sound like a burden, I got the feeling that Miss Cooley was actually looking forward to finding out the answer herself.

GE markets a line of freezers under the Hotpoint brand name, so I asked for information about those models as well. "I'll be glad to check on the Hotpoint models for you," Miss Cooley said.

What was with her? It was 2:00 A.M. in Louisville, where she was answering my call. How could she be so GLAD to help me?

She talked me through the various features, and then she offered to look up a nearby dealer where I could compare several models.

I know that GE makes fine products, and I appreciate being able to get information whenever I want it, even if that's late at night. The icing on the cake is the extremely congenial way Miss Cooley and her colleagues respond to callers' questions.

The GE Answer Center is one outstanding example of a company's commitment to providing customers with complete, accurate information and friendly human contact. One of General Electric's original reasons for establishing the Answer Center was to "put on a friendly face" for consumers who might perceive GE as a gigantic, cold, bureaucratic corporation.

What struck me most during my conversation with Miss Cooley was something very simple: her consistent use of phrases like "I'll be glad to check that . . ." and "I'll be happy to get that information." In each case she communicated not just that she had or would get the information I needed, but that she'd do it with pleasure. Imagine working an eight-hour shift beside Miss Cooley. If you handle twelve calls an hour, and each one includes, on average, three requests for information, you have the opportunity to choose between saying, "I'll **have to** look that up" and "I'll be **glad to** look that up," 288 times each day. After hearing yourself say "I'll have to" 288 times in a single workshift, how are you likely to feel? Exhausted, cranky, weary, put-upon? Would it make a difference if you kept hearing yourself say, "I'll be glad to" instead?

Indeed, it can make a big difference, as the training staff and management at GE can attest. Even after answering thousands of calls, GE staffers there are remarkably enthusiastic, cheerful, and at the same time entirely professional. One reason for the excellent morale is the training department's focus on Power Talking. From their first day in training, new employees are coached to deliver accurate information in an upbeat manner.

In the course of an average day, we all respond to many requests for information. A simple word substitution changes the whole tone of the response. Saying "I'll be **glad to** check those dates for you" not only projects a pleasant, cooperative attitude; it also makes you feel better.

Whether you're responsible for employee training programs in your organization or are interested in making your own dealings with friends, supervisors, or customers more rewarding, take advantage of the benefits that result from substituting positive phrases like "I'll be happy to" for burdensome ones like "I'll have to."

QUICK REFERENCE

What you can do right now:
Each time you begin to say "I'll **have to**," substitute a phrase that shows you'll be **glad to.** Notice the difference it makes in your own mood and in others' attitudes about cooperating with you.

Instead of saying,

"I'm afraid I'll have to check that and call you back."

Say,

"I'd like to check that and call you back."

Instead of saying,

"I'm gonna have to pull your file."

Say,

"I'll be glad to pull your file."

Instead of saying,

"I'll have to do it."

Say,

"I'll be glad to do it."

2. Will You Try, or Will You DO It?

Your garage has been a mess for months. Tools are jumbled on the workbench, the recycling bins are overflowing, and the floor is filthy. Your spouse asks you (again) to clean it up this weekend.

Say out loud to yourself:

"OK, OK, I'll try to do it before the ball game on Sunday."

Now say:

"I will have it cleaned up by Sunday afternoon."

Which promise will motivate you to follow through with action?

Jeff Salzman is the co-author of *Real World 101* and *Career Tracking*, both valuable guides for accelerating your success in business. He told me about an encounter with a lawyer that dramatized the difference between "I'll try" and "I will."

Early in Jeff's advertising career, one of his clients was sued. The plaintiff's lawyer wanted Jeff to give a deposition. "The game," Jeff points out, "is to make yourself as unavailable as possible so as to avoid helping the other side build its case." The lawyer asked if Monday would be convenient for Jeff to meet with him. Jeff was busy. How about Tuesday? Oh, gosh, meetings all day. The lawyer quickly realized that Jeff was being cagey, so he switched gears, asking an open-ended question: "So, Jeff, when will you give your deposition?" Jeff couldn't maintain that he was "too busy" forever, so he suggested, "I'll try for two weeks from Friday." The lawyer's response was to ask for a firm commitment: "Do I have your word that you **will** give your deposition two weeks from Friday?" Jeff thought to himself, "He's got me! Once I've made a commitment and given my word, he's won the game." Of course, Jeff honored his commitment. And he also learned a lesson. Ever since that phone call, whenever he detects an indefinite "I'll try . . ." in somebody's statement, he counters with, "Do I have your word that you **will**?"

The person who benefits most when you say "I will" is *you.* When you hear yourself making a firm commitment, you are more likely to follow through with action than if you say "I'll try." That's merely an abbreviated form of "I'll give it a shot but I'm not making any promises—we'll just wait and see what happens." Or, as Drs. Ken Blanchard and Norman Vincent Peale wrote in *The Power of Ethical Management,* "Trying is just a noisy way of not doing something."

QUICK REFERENCE

What you can do right now:
Tell yourself and everyone else what you **will** do, not what you'll **try** to do.

Instead of saying,

"I'll try to finish up the market research analysis by the middle of the week."

Say,

"I will complete the market research analysis no later than Wednesday afternoon."

Instead of saying,

"I'll try to practice my pitching three times a week to get ready for the softball league playoffs next month."

Say,

"I will practice my pitching three times a week and be ready for the softball league playoffs next month."

Instead of saying,

"I'll try to do it."

Say,

"I will do it."

3. Say What You Want to Do

While handling your arrangements for a last-minute business trip, your travel agent suggests guaranteeing the hotel room with a credit card.

Say out loud to yourself:

"I'd hate to see you lose your reservation if the flight is delayed and the hotel assumes you're a no-show."

Now say:

"I want to guarantee that your room will be held for you even if you arrive a little later than expected."

Which version sounds more helpful? Which suggests a more optimistic outlook?

You hear some interesting excuses when you're an Accounts Receivable collector. I was coaching a seasoned collector named Sharon at Ford Motor Credit's Detroit branch office when we encountered Leon D. This customer insisted that he was deceased, and had even personally signed a letter verifying his own demise!

Sharon showed me the extensive records of her previous conversations with Leon D., and his case was very sad indeed. He had purchased a new Ford pickup truck and financed it through his dealer. Soon after his loan was approved, he developed a severe brain tumor that clouded his thinking. Sharon had verified his diagnosis with the Veterans Administration hospital and learned that his condition was life-threatening. Since it was impossible to reason with Leon, she called his wife and learned that he was on strong medication, and was drinking heavily and behaving irrationally.

I listened in as Sharon called Leon's wife at her workplace:

> "Hello, Mrs. D., this is Sharon at Ford Motor Credit. I'm calling because we still haven't received the overdue payments for your husband's truck, and now his record in the computer shows that his insurance has been canceled for nonpayment. I hate to say it, but I see no alternative but to have the vehicle repossessed unless you're willing to help me."

Sharon had already threatened Leon with repossession, and his response was to hide the vehicle. Repo agents had been driving by his house looking for the truck, but were unable to locate it. If Mrs. D. wouldn't make the payments, Sharon hoped that she would at least reveal the truck's location.

Unfortunately, Mrs. D. wasn't helpful:

> *"Go ahead and do whatever you have to do. I can't talk with him. He's completely crazy. I have no influence over that man. Take the truck if that's what you want to do."*

Sharon pressed on and described the likely consequences:

"Mrs. D., a repossession is going to look very bad on your credit record and will be part of your file for years to come. You don't want to have a default, do you?"

Mrs. D. knew that she wasn't legally responsible.

"Listen, young lady, I didn't sign that contract and I'm not accountable for Leon's irresponsible behavior. There's nothing I'm going to do to help you and I don't care what happens. Besides, the doctors say he's going to die any day. I have no money to pay you or anybody else. I'm barely able to make the house payments. But Leon does have an insurance policy. And when he dies, that's my only hope of keeping my home. I don't drive his truck, and I didn't sign for it, so why should I care what happens to it?"

Now, with all the cards on the table, Sharon didn't know what to say. She ended her conversation having made no headway at all:

"Mrs. D., it sounds like you have enough problems to deal with. I'd hate to see them get worse because of a repossession and default on your husband's credit records, but if you won't help me, that's my only choice at this point."

After the call, Sharon and I talked about the difference between an "I'd hate to . . ." and an "I want to . . ." approach. People don't care to hear about potential bad news—in fact, they'll screen it out. They reach a point where they think things simply cannot get any worse. Sharon's approach had this effect on Mrs. D.

She had been unsuccessful using the negative strategy: "If you don't act now, things will get even worse." I suggested that Sharon use the positive "I want to . . ." strategy rather than the negative "I'd hate to . . ." approach which hadn't been working.

The following week Sharon called Mrs. D. again:

"Mrs. D., I can understand the uncomfortable position you're in considering your husband's poor health and difficult behavior. My aim is to make things better for you, not worse. You're absolutely right, you have no legal responsibility to help me locate the truck for repossession. I can help you avoid a potential problem. Because of your husband's canceled auto insurance coverage, medical history, and drinking behavior, it's very likely that you would be sued if he injured or, heaven forbid, killed someone while driving the truck. I want to help you keep your home and make sure you receive your insurance proceeds. What I *can* do is ensure that Leon doesn't injure anyone. If you'll tell me where to find the truck, I'll have it quietly removed and will tell nobody about our conversation. I feel sorry about the terrible situation you're in, and I want to help make it better."

Mrs. D. hadn't thought of it that way. She quickly agreed to tell Sharon where Leon had the truck hidden and asked that she arrange to have it picked up as soon as possible.

As a precaution, Sharon phoned the local police department and explained that Ford was about to repossess the vehicle. The cops knew Leon well, and considered him extremely dangerous. The Chief of Police insisted on helping out by sending three of his patrol cars to rendezvous with Sharon and the repo agent. Ford avoided a "write-off" on the vehicle, and they may well have saved a good deal of grief for Mrs. D. and for potential innocent victims, too. The "I want to . . ." approach helped Sharon make the best of a bad situation.

Whenever you're motivating someone to do what you'd like them to do, focus on the desirable positive end result, not the negative potential. Tell people what you **want to** do for them, not what you'd **hate to** do to them.

You face many opportunities to make this simple substitution throughout your daily life. If you and your spouse are planning to attend the school play, and you're concerned about tight timing, you generate more positive attention by saying:

> "Let's both leave work a little early today. I **want** to be sure we're both there on time to enjoy Emily's performance in the school play,"

rather than,

> "You'd better leave work a little early today. I'd **hate to** have you get caught in traffic and **miss** Emily's performance in the school play."

If you're talking with a sales prospect about a special offer that expires at the end of the month, consider the more positive impact you will have by saying:

> "I **want to be** sure we get your order processed before Friday so you can take advantage of the special bonus program running this month,"

instead of using the negative "hate to" approach:

> "I'd **hate to** see you **miss** the special bonus program we're running this month, so you'd better be sure your order isn't late."

Whenever you use a phrase like "I'd hate to," you focus attention on the looming potential negative outcome you want to avoid. The image you project will be a positive one when you focus on the good results you are moving toward, rather than the bad ones you seek to avoid.

QUICK REFERENCE

What you can do right now:
Use "I want to" and describe the positive outcomes you envision, rather than saying what you'd "hate to" have happen.
  Instead of saying,

  "We'd better go to the airport a little early. I'd hate to miss the flight because we got caught in traffic."

Say,

"Let's go to the airport a little early. I want to be sure we make the flight in plenty of time."

Instead of saying,

  "I'd hate to see your credit ruined by having your car repossessed and your account shown as a default."

Say,

"I want to help you keep your credit record strong and ensure that your account shows a positive rating."

Instead of saying,

  "I'd hate to give you the wrong information."

Say,

"I want to give you the right information."

4. I Haven't Yet and I CAN

Your boss asks you to prepare a Lotus spreadsheet analysis and determine the company's present break-even production level. You're not proficient with Lotus 1-2-3 or any similar spreadsheet software.

Say out loud to yourself:

"I can't do a spreadsheet analysis and I can't even figure out Lotus 1-2-3."

Now, say:

"I haven't done a spreadsheet analysis before. I can start by learning to use Lotus 1-2-3."

Which sounds like the employee who's going to move ahead, learn new skills, and become an increasingly valuable asset to her company? Which lacks confidence, sounds stagnant, and probably faces a limited future in this position?

As Beth, my new hairstylist, began lathering up the peppermint shampoo, she started in with the usual get-friendly-with-your-new-client opening question:

"So, George, what business are you in?"

Most people don't know any professional speakers, so I wasn't surprised at her reaction when I told her about my work:

"What do you mean? You give speeches for a living? Oh gawd, I can't speak. Oh, I'm OK just one-on-one, but it would be impossible for me to give a speech. In fact, one of my teachers had me do all my oral book reports in writing because I just couldn't talk in front of the class. I even took a speech course once, but I got an F. I get all sweaty and my mind goes completely blank. No, I can't give speeches."

Each time the subject of speaking has come up since her first oral book report, Beth has repeated to herself and anyone listening: "I can't give a speech." Her mind has heard her own proclamation over and over again, and she's absolutely convinced it's true.

Beth talked (nonstop) through my shampoo, cut, and style, so I know she **can** speak. If there had been fifty other clients waiting for their haircuts, all within earshot but out of sight, Beth would have been giving a speech without even knowing it.

To be accurate, she should have said,

"I haven't ever liked giving speeches."

Or, even,

"I don't like giving speeches, have always done poorly in the past, and don't want to ever do it again. In fact, I feel scared stiff at the prospect of facing a group of people and giving a speech."

That might all be true, but for Beth to say she **can't** speak in front of a group is inaccurate and self-limiting.

There's very little that you or I absolutely can't do. I've never competed in Alaska's annual Iditarod dogsled race, don't like prolonged exposure to subzero temperatures, and do my best to avoid pain and suffering. I **can,** though, compete in a dogsled race across Alaska. Of course, I'd need years of training, an extensive and demanding physical conditioning program, substantial financial backing, and lots of other preparation; and I **can** compete in the Iditarod race. I don't want to and guarantee that I won't. But I **can.**

Whenever people tell you—or themselves—what they **can't** do, they're slamming shut the door that leads to their untapped potential. As I wrote this book, I often caught myself saying what it seemed like I **couldn't** do. On many mornings I looked over my daily journal of writing progress and thought to myself,

"I can't squeeze out more than two and a half or three hours of solid writing each day. At this rate I can't possibly finish the manuscript before my publisher's deadline."

Well, you're reading the book and I did complete it on time. The correct statement would have been:

"I haven't yet exceeded three uninterrupted hours in my daily writing schedule. I am going to finish the manuscript on time, so that means I'll need to write for about six hours each day. Starting today, I can begin adjusting my personal schedule and free up more time for concentrated writing."

When someone says, "I can't do that," it's probable that he's placing an inaccurate and counterproductive limitation on what he can accomplish. The word "can't" acts as a self-fulfilling future predictor. If you say you can't accomplish something, that's like saying you never will. Since your mind likes you to be right, it works hard to ensure that you're correct when you say you "can't." It functions as a powerful saboteur, undermining your effectiveness so you do not reach your goals, even if you attempt to do so.

QUICK REFERENCE

What you can do right now:
When describing your capabilities to yourself or to someone else, eliminate "I can't" from your vocabulary.

Instead of saying,

"I can't even break par on that golf course!"

Say,

"I haven't yet broken par, and I'm working on it."

Instead of saying,

"There's no point looking at new homes. We can't even afford a condo! We'll be renting some lousy apartment for the rest of our lives."

Say,

"Considering our present financial situation, we can afford a home in two or three years. As the market adjusts, we'll be saving toward our down payment. Meanwhile, we can fine-tune our budget."

Instead of saying,

"I can't do that."

Say,

"I haven't yet done it and I can."

5. *Refuse to Be Helpless*

After you've been feeling tired for months, your doctor discovers that you have a rare bone-marrow disease. Following an extensive course of treatment that includes hundreds of transfusions, the doctor tells you that there is nothing further medical science can do to prolong your life.

Say out loud to yourself:

"I guess that's it. If the doctors hold out no hope for me, I may as well quit. What's the point? I'm in pain and I'm going to die anyway. I give up."

Now, say:

"I don't accept that. My condition is not hopeless. I can and I will improve the quality, if not the quantity, of my life."

Which sounds like the patient who will see little improvement in his condition? Who has a fighting chance?

Michael Ballard's "new life" began when his doctor, George P. Konok, M.D., said,

"I'm going to start your treatment from the neck down. You're going to finish it from the neck up."

Michael was a successful account executive in Ontario, Canada, selling packaged goods through the network of Hallmark stores in his territory. He became ill and was diagnosed as having inflammatory bowel disease, commonly known as colitis. Some of the unpleasant effects are emotional: worry, panic, and embarrassment. It doesn't do much for your self-confidence to know that you could "have an accident" at any time. The worst part was hearing a well-intentioned medical professional tell him, "There is nothing that can be done for your condition."

Colitis can have a particularly sinister consequence: It is often a precursor to cancer. Soon, Michael was diagnosed with cancer of the bowel near his liver. The doctors warned that his lymph glands could be next, and for cancer patients, that's usually the beginning of the end.

Along with this new diagnosis came a blessing in the form of his new physician, Dr. Konok. He pulled a blackboard up to Michael's bedside and gave him a serious "chalk talk," diagramming the various organs that were affected, showing

Michael what the surgeons would do and explaining how the chemotherapy was supposed to work. After a careful, factual explanation of Michael's current condition, he got around to the prognosis. He flipped the chalk up in the air and said,

> **"I can tell you the odds that are in the medical text-books, but I want you to know that you make your own odds. I cannot guarantee that you can make yourself live any longer. I can absolutely guarantee that you can live a fuller life if you decide to. When you begin your chemotherapy, you will experience side effects. If you view this as a healing process, you will have a much better experience than if you view it as a sickening one. I will treat you from the neck down. Your job is to treat yourself from the neck up."**

Michael's treatment proceeded, with three operations. After the third, supposedly final step in his course of treatment, he was informed that the operation had failed; the cancer was still proliferating.

Michael had always used positive language in his professional life. Now, though, facing the biggest "contest" of his life, he was using negative language, accepting the doctors' assessments that his situation was "hopeless." When they said, "You can't change things," he believed them.

At this point, Michael Ballard decided that the same techniques which had brought him success in his sales contests were his best hope for success in his life.

Home from the hospital between treatments, he bought a new pair of running shoes to use as he became well again. He played positive music including "The Rainbow Connection" and the theme from "Rocky." He paced around the house in his new running shoes, reading favorite quotations from *The Best of Success*. Michael's breakthrough came when he transferred the skills he had learned, mastered, and benefited from in business to his personal health.

Today his doctor describes Michael Ballard as "Dangerously fit. Able to leap tall buildings with a single bound, and very tall ones with a running start."

He had had no sign of cancer for eight years, and has chosen not to have any for the balance of his life.

Michael Ballard now has a new profession. He teaches seminars about using the power of language to help patients recover from their illnesses. He's intent on making doctors and nurses acutely aware of how damaging their language can be for worried patients—and how powerfully helpful it can be when used positively.

He explains that the techniques and specific words he used won't work for everyone. In his volunteer work, patients often comment,

"Michael, I can't say what you said. It doesn't feel right for me."

He answers,

"Fine, put it in your own words, but keep the spirit. Repeat the positive affirmations that feel right for you. If you say nothing else, say 'Oh, yes I can.' Don't let anyone, medical professional or not, tell you that your situation is hopeless. You can always improve the quality of your life, even if you don't change the quantity of it."

If you are already threatened by a serious illness, please do not give up. You can fight. Your positive expectations will improve the quality of your life.

QUICK REFERENCE

What you can do right now:
If you feel sick, supplement prudent medical attention with personal action. Using your language to promote a positive

attitude and strengthen your body's natural disease-fighting powers.

Instead of saying,

"I can't fight this. My condition is hopeless. The doctor said so."

Say,

"I can improve the quality of my life, and I will. The doctor doesn't realize how strong I am."

Instead of saying,

"My condition is hopeless; I can't change it."

Say,

"I can improve the quality of my life."

6. Better When Than If

Your child is unenthusiastic about his French classes and has a hard time completing his homework assignment each night. Tonight you use a reward to encourage him to finish.

Say out loud to yourself:

"If you finish your French assignment tonight, you may have a big helping of that new French Vanilla ice cream I bought today.

Now, say:

"When you finish your French assignment tonight, we'll all have a big helping of that new French Vanilla ice cream I bought today."

Which sounds like you really expect him to finish his homework? Which shows that you aren't at all sure he's going to?

You've probably noticed merchants in your neighborhood becoming more environmentally conscious lately. Some of the supermarkets in our community post special tags indicating products that use recycled packaging, those that are biodegradable, and so on. Some of the stores offer a few cents off your total bill when you bring in your own shopping bag. Some have a small bin for depositing shopping bags to be recycled. All those shopping bags are menacing to our environment because they can last for centuries. Recycling also saves trees and oil.

As I began writing this book, our local Safeway store made no provision for recycling shoppers' bags. My wife decided to change that. She said to the checkout clerk, "I really appreciate the efforts you've made to be environmentally conscious. When will you begin a shopping-bag recycling program?"

Not, "do you think you could," not ''would you consider," not "it might be a nice idea if you would." "WHEN WILL YOU?"

The clerk responded:

"Good question. I'm going to talk to the manager myself before the end of my shift. We should have a bag recycling program. It won't take long to set it up."

The Coal Creek Village Safeway store now has a shopping bag recycling bin. If your supermarket doesn't yet, ask a "When Question," not an "If Question" next time you're shopping.

• • •

When Citibank, US West, Bank of America, and AT&T want to improve their bill collectors' effectiveness, they call in Bill Arnold, principal of the International Collection Training Institute. His job is to show people how they can project positive expectations onto others. Consider the difference between saying,

> "I'll tell you what: If you can pay this balance off by the end of the week, I'll waive the late charges."

and

> **"Bring in your check for $67.50 before the end of the week, and I will waive your late charges. When before Friday will you come in so I can credit your account?"**

Bill steps right beyond the typical question, "Do you think you could possibly pay this off by the end of the week?" He projects the positive expectation that the debtor will pay. His goal is to finalize the schedule for doing so, not to find out **if** it's going to happen.

If the debtor says, "Wait a minute, here. I didn't say I was going to pay by the end of the week," Bill backtracks to establish the basis for his positive expectation:

> **"Richard, I'm sure you are an honest and responsible person, aren't you?"**
> **"Of course I am."**
> **"And you do want to honor your obligations, don't you?"**
> **"Well, I do want to."**
> **"So you'd like to settle this by the end of the week, wouldn't you?"**
> **"Yes, but I don't have enough money right now."**

Once again Bill steps past the "iffy" questions and projects a positive expectation. Rather than saying,

"Well, when do you think you might have enough to pay it off?"

he presumes that the debtor wants to make headway as quickly as possible. He asks,

"How much are you going to be short of the \$_____ that's due on this week's payment?"

In other words, Bill doesn't take the approach of asking **if** the debtor will pay, he moves ahead to the next question, **when** will he pay? And if the debtor says he doesn't have enough to pay it all now, Bill doesn't ask when he will, he asks **how much** he **will** pay right now.

When you want someone to take a reasonable action, ask a logistical question. Not "if," but ''when and how much?"

QUICK REFERENCE

What you can do right now:
When you hear yourself starting to ask a conditional "If . . ." question, rephrase it to incorporate your positive expectation.

Instead of saying,

"We like the new park area you've provided for the homeowners in our development, but it's awfully rocky. We're wondering if it would be possible to have the rocks removed and the surface smoothed?"

Say,

"We like the new park area you've provided for the homeowners in our development. When will you have the rocks removed and the surface smoothed?"

Instead of saying,

"I know your repair people are probably really busy, but we need our phones fixed quickly. Do you think you could send someone over sometime today?"

Say,

"I know your repair people are really busy and I appreciate your help. Since these phones are our crucial link to customers, we need them repaired fast. What time this afternoon can you have someone here?"

Instead of saying,

"I was wondering if you can . . .?"

Say,

"When will you . . .?"

7. It's No Problem!

You've just been informed that you were "volunteered" to act as a chaperone for the Youth Activity Program offered in conjunction with your spouse's professional association convention next month.

Say out loud to yourself:

"Sixty teenagers in one room, and I'm going to be responsible for maintaining order? That's going to be a terrible problem!"

Now, say:

"Sixty teenagers in one room, and I'm going to be responsible for maintaining order? That's going to be an interesting challenge!"

Which version presupposes that things will go poorly? Which suggests that you'll work out a creative way to handle the situation?

The Master of Ceremonies introduced Sonny Hendrix as he wheeled himself to center stage to deliver his commencement address. Everyone in the audience could see that Sonny's body was somewhat asymmetrical, his arms and legs positioned oddly as he sat in his wheelchair. He didn't hold his head up quite straight, and there was something unusual about the way he spoke. Many in the audience must have been thinking, "And I thought I had problems. Sonny's entire existence in that wheelchair must be one big problem."

Sonny doesn't see it that way.

I met him at the most inspiring graduation ceremony I've ever attended. It took place at the Resource Center for the Handicapped, or R.C.H., near my home in Seattle. A former elementary school facility, deemed unnecessary several years ago, has been converted to a learning center dedicated solely to the needs of people with special physical challenges.

R.C.H. students are not content to receive public assistance and idly waste their lives. They decide to be active, contributing members of the work force and enroll in rigorous business and vocational courses with the aim of securing employment and becoming self-sufficient. The program is supported entirely by corporate sponsors and volunteers.

The Commencement Program began with guest speakers representing a few of the corporations that support the Center: The Boeing Company, John Fluke Manufacturing, GTE, Digital Equipment Corporation, and so on. Not one speaker during the entire evening's program used the word "problem." It would have been so easy to describe these students as people beset with multiple problems: limited mobility, public ignorance, stares and scrutiny, and many forms of prejudice.

Nobody mentioned "problems." They all talked about "challenges." Frank Shrontz, Chairman and CEO of Boeing, noted that his company employs 10,000 people with "medical challenges" rather than "disabilities." Instead of referring to the graduates as people whose "problems" entitle them to pity or special considerations, he pointed out that Boeing's hiring policies have been formulated to address the company's own best interests. "When we find individuals like these people, who have overcome significant challenges, we see people who have courage and perseverance. They make great employees."

Sonny Hendrix was one of the student speakers. He had completed the Center's "TeleProfessionals" curriculum, emphasizing telemarketing and customer-service telephone skills. Addressing his fellow graduates, speaking into the microphone that was being held for him beside his wheelchair, he said:

"Our disabilities are only equal to the barriers or doors we allow to be placed in front of us. We are responsible for our challenges."

Sonny wasn't willing to accept the notion that a handicapped person faces problems and that most doors are closed to him. After the ceremony I phoned him for an interview and we talked about "problems" and "challenges." He made a very distinct differentiation:

"A problem is something you hate. A challenge is something you want to overcome."

One of my clients is a midlevel manager at a large telephone company. She noticed that her first-level supervisors brought their "problems" to her, asking for her solutions.

This practice wasn't helping to prepare them for career advancement, and left her with little time to handle her other responsibilities. She wanted to maintain her "open door" policy, and she noticed that when she was very accessible, she'd often reach the end of the day feeling that she'd been "dumped on" all day long and had accomplished little except for extinguishing many small fires.

Her solution for this "problem" was to meet with all the supervisors who reported to her and institute a new "solution policy." She reaffirmed her desire to talk with supervisors individually whenever they felt the need. However, she asked that they change their dialogue. Supervisors were forbidden to use the work "problem," and were also prohibited from starting the discussion until they had at least one solution in mind.

The old way:

"Excuse me, Kathryn, I need to talk with you. I have a problem with Dennis Swall. He'd been late for three days in a row now, and he's setting a very bad example for others. What should I do about it?"

The new way:

"Excuse me, Kathryn, I'd like to tell you about a situation I'm handling. I've had a challenge improving Dennis Swall's punctuality, and I have an idea for how to handle it. Please tell me if you can suggest an even more effective approach."

The result? Kathryn did her supervisors a great service by encouraging them to be self-reliant. She was still able to ensure that the solutions they wanted to implement were appropriate, and everyone felt less depressed. Rather than being inundated with burdensome "problems," Kathryn and her supervisors used their meetings to discuss the relative merits of various positive solutions.

The same problem/solution substitution will work in your

personal life, too. When friends or family members start talking about "problems," help them by shifting the discussion toward solutions. This keeps you focused on challenging opportunities rather than on depressing problems.

QUICK REFERENCE

What you can do right now:
Substitute "challenge" or "opportunity" for "problem" and concentrate on exploring solutions.

Instead of saying,

> "Now that Jason is a teenager, we're having all kinds of problems with him."

Say,

> **"We face some new challenges, now that Jason is a teenager."**

Instead of saying,

> "The recent international crises have disrupted the currency exchange markets and caused all kinds of problems."

Say,

> **"These recent currency fluctuations have opened up lots of new opportunities."**

Instead of saying,

> "I'm afraid that's going to be a problem."

Say,

> **"That sounds like a challenging opportunity."**

8. Self-Fulfilling Prophecies Come True

After finally becoming adept with the telephone system used in your division, you're transferred to another building, where a totally different system is used.

Say out loud to yourself:

"Oh no! I'm terrible at learning all these phone features. It'll probably take me months to get up to speed, if I ever do. It was bad enough retrieving voice mail and making transfers from my old phone. I'll never learn a whole new system of commands."

Now, say:

"I became proficient with the phones we used before, and I know I can do just as well with the new system. I'll get some coaching from my co-workers, and pick up one of those quick-reference cards to keep handy."

Which sounds like someone who is doomed to cutting off callers and bumbling transfers with his new phone? Who's going to apply himself and learn the new system quickly?

Somehow, over the last few years, I have convinced myself that I'm terrible with directions. The curious thing is that I've traveled extensively throughout much of the world without ever getting lost. I've hitchhiked from Nairobi to Cape Town, trekked into the Highlands of New Guinea, and hiked ancient unmarked Inca trails in the Andes. I always reached my intended destination without problems.

Yet I've recently become notorious for getting lost right in my own hometown. Our friends Lou and Vanna Novak recently invited us to dinner at their home, just 25 minutes

away from ours. Before leaving the house, I called Vanna
and said,

> "I realize we've been to your place twice before, but I
> think you'd better give me the directions again. You know
> how I'm always getting lost."

As I went through the motions of writing down her instructions, I didn't take the trouble to verify the details, expecting that I'd get lost anyway. Sure enough, half an hour
after we were due for dinner, I called on the car phone.

> "Lou, we're lost. I have no idea what happened. I watched
> for the Magnolia Street Bridge, just like Vanna said, but
> somehow we ended up on the Ballard Bridge, and now
> I'm not even sure which side of the canal we're supposed
> to be on. I always get lost coming to your house."

I felt so foolish. Our infant daughter was screaming in her
car seat, and my wife, Julie, was in the backseat, tending to
the baby and chastising me for garbling Vanna's instructions. We finally arrived (45 minutes late) only after Lou
"talked me in" on the car phone as I drove. It was like one of
those old-fashioned movie scenes where the pilot of a small
plane has a heart attack and his passenger guides the plane in
for a landing by listening to radioed instructions from the
tower.

On the way home, Julie pointed out that, right from the
start, I had set myself up for getting lost. There was no way I
wouldn't get lost. I'd programmed Lou and Vanna **and myself** for the eventual outcome by saying, "I'm always getting
lost."

I have a compass in the van, I'm smart, I carry a detailed
map, and I'm a skilled communicator. There's no logical reason for me to ever get lost. Why create artificial limitations
on my own abilities? As of right now, I've decided to stop
saying, "I always get lost." Instead, I'll listen carefully to instructions, make clear notes, and say, "I'll find it easily."

What are your self-imposed limitations? What have you convinced yourself you're not good at? What myths do you perpetuate by telling others you lack certain talents?

"I'm all thumbs when it comes to fixing things."
"I can't cook worth a darn."
"Study French? I can't even pronounce the names of California wines. I'm terrible with languages."

I have decided today, as I write, that I'm unlocking my talent for finding my way anywhere. I invite you to decide, today, as you read this page, to unlock more of your talents, too. Stop telling yourself and others that you're "not good at" something, and find out how good you truly are.

QUICK REFERENCE

What you can do right now:
Replace habitual self-limiting phrases with empowering assertions.

Instead of saying,

"I've always had trouble with math. I'm just not good with numbers. I can never figure out percentages, even with a calculator."

Say,

"I do lots of mathematical things well. I'm going to stop at the library and refresh myself on some basic calculations I've forgotten, like figuring out percentages."

Instead of saying,

"I'm no good at that."

Say,

"I'm betting better at that."

9. Get a Return on Your Investments

You sell advertising space for a leading nature magazine, and are meeting with an entrepreneur who has decided to market a special high-tech birdfeeder. Hers is a shoestring operation, and the potential advertiser has just started her business, operating from her kitchen table.

Say out loud to yourself:

"I realize that spending $500 on a magazine ad is a big commitment. It's hard to tell, of course, but you could get hundreds of orders."

Now, say:

"This ad represents a $500 investment. Let's look at the return that will generate even if the response is only one-half of one percent of our readers."

Which approach is most likely to catch the entrepreneur's interest? Which sounds like the wiser allocation of funds?

Since I recently became a father, I've been advised by many other parents to "spend as much time as possible" with my child while she's still very young. Sometimes, major parts of my day pass when I've done nothing except play with, talk to, adore, and love our little baby. My wife does the same. I don't think of it as "spending" time with her. We're "investing" our time. I enjoy a big return: I know I'm a happier, more productive person when I take time out to enjoy Kelcie, and I also believe that for her whole lifetime, she'll benefit from getting a high quantity of high-quality attention from her parents.

There may be times as you read this book when you think I'm making too big of a deal about semantics. This could be one of those times. Consider the important influence your words have on your thinking.

Let's start with *Webster's Ninth New Collegiate Dictionary*:

> **spend:** 1: to use up or pay out : EXPEND 2a: EXHAUST, WEAR OUT 2b: to consume wastefully : SQUANDER 3: to cause or permit to elapse : PASS 4: GIVE UP, SACRIFICE

My goodness, is that what I'm doing when I take a break and play with Kelcie for an hour? Waste, squander, sacrifice? Now, let's flip back to the "I"s.

> **invest:** 1: to commit (money) in order to earn a financial return 2: to make use of for future benefits or advantages

That's more like it. When I use my time to be with my daughter, I'm doing it because I expect benefits and advantages. I get to feel good and so does she.

Are you investing enough time with your family? Would the "payoff" be worth increasing your stake?

In business, when you decide to commit your limited funds to buy computers, hire people, or pay rent, you do it because you expect the company to get a return on its investment. You don't spend on advertising, promotion, health care programs, and company vehicles—you invest.

Consider substituting "invest" for "spend" in your personal life. I've found there are quite a few times when "spending" is appropriate. If I go the the State Fair and purchase some cotton candy, I'm not making an investment. I do buy things just because I like them for the moment. However, when it comes to buying a car, or choosing which washing machine to buy, or adding to my wardrobe, I like to think of my purchases as "investments."

Thinking—and talking—about "investing" creates a consciousness of plenty rather than scarcity. If you're always spending, you're continually depleting limited resources.

When you invest, you apply some of your resources with the expectation that you'll create more of them.

When you describe how you'll use your time, money, and energy, talk in terms of investing. Use your resources in a wise way that will generate a payback, whether that means short-term satisfaction, long-term financial rewards, or a deep sense of having done the right thing.

QUICK REFERENCE

What you can do right now:
Substitute "invest" for "spend" when you talk about how you'll use your time, money, and other resources.

Instead of saying,

> "We're going to spend more money on our house and add a greenhouse enclosure outside the kitchen windows."

Say,

> **"We're going to invest in a greenhouse enclosure to make our home more enjoyable. When we move, it'll be an attractive selling feature, too."**

Instead of saying,

> "We just cannot spend any more money on furniture right now. Your department is going to have to make do with desks and chairs we already have."

Say,

> **"We're not going to purchase any new furniture at this time. While investing in more ergonomic chairs and tables could result in higher productivity, some other investments will provide a better return for us right now."**

Instead of saying,

"With fall approaching, it's time to spend another bundle on clothes. I need a new coat, new shoes, and while I'm at it, I'll have to buy some new slacks, too."

Say,

"I'm going to invest in a new wardrobe for fall and winter. I'll choose a good coat to keep me warm and comfortable, and some shoes and slacks to help me look my best at work."

Instead of saying,

"I'm going to spend some time and money taking night classes."

Say,

"I'm going to invest some time and money taking night classes so I'm ready to move ahead in my career."

10. Nothing's Impossible

You've already had a terrific sales record and your performance is nearly 20% ahead of the same period last year. The Regional Manager compliments you on your performance and informs you that your quota for the next quarter has just been increased by 25%.

Say out loud to yourself:

"That's impossible! I'm cranking at top speed already, and I got lucky on a few big orders in the first quarter.

That's why I'm 20% ahead of quota right now. There's no way I can close the year with a 25% increase."

Now, say:

"That's going to be a challenge. A combination of circumstances has helped to make my 20% gain possible so far. You can continue relying on my total commitment for the second half of the year. I'll do my best to meet the new quota, and I don't believe that the 25% increase is realistic."

Which sounds like the person who has a shot at hitting 25%?

You may be familiar with one of Reverend Robert Schuller's many books, or perhaps you watch his television broadcasts from the Crystal Cathedral in California. I was fortunate to be among the architecture buffs who toured the Cathedral when its designer, Philip Johnson, officially unveiled his gem to the architectural community. I later learned the "inside story" behind the construction of this impressive edifice.

When he first called Philip Johnson, Dr. Schuller explained that he wanted to build a dramatic cathedral constructed entirely of glass, with outstanding acoustics and an unobstructed view of the pulpit from every single seat. This kind of building had never been constructed before, and required vast amounts of special glass and innovative construction techniques. On top of that, the Southern California site is located in one of the world's most active earthquake zones. As he explained his vision of the Crystal Cathedral to Mr. Johnson, Dr. Schuller added one special challenge: He had no money.

Mr. Johnson looked at him and said,

"Wait a minute, let me get this straight. You want to erect a huge building the likes of which the world has never seen. You want it to be constructed using materials and techniques never before employed, and you have absolutely no money to work with? That's impossible!"

Smiling, Reverend Schuller asked Philip Johnson to open the large dictionary atop a pedestal in his office and look up the word "impossible." Mr. Johnson walked across the room, began flipping pages, and after a moment of confusion, the famous architect looked up and said, "There's no 'impossible' in this dictionary."

There was Dr. Schuller, standing beside his desk wearing an impish grin and holding an X-Acto knife in his uplifted hand. He explained to the puzzled architect that he uses his blade to remove that negative word from any dictionary that crosses his path.

"Anything is possible," says Dr. Schuller.

There are very few things you may set out to accomplish that are truly "impossible." Difficult, demanding, challenging, never-before-achieved, sure—but not impossible. Why prejudice your own expectations by labeling a lofty pursuit as "impossible"?

Most of the great figures in history have had little use for the word "impossible." Did Columbus say it was impossible to sail to another continent? Did Kennedy say it was impossible to put an American astronaut on the moon? They faced daunting initial challenges and many setbacks along the way. And they decided to not label their goals as "impossible."

The single worst effect of deciding that something is "impossible" is that you don't even give your efforts a chance. The principle of "cognitive dissonance" applies to the use of the word "impossible." Your mind likes to make sure you're right. When you've convinced yourself that a thing is so, you set about to prove it.

If you tell yourself that it's impossible to awaken an hour early and work on setting up a realistic family budget, it is.

You sleep a little too long, you feel groggy rather than alert, and you decide to put off working on the budget until some other time. Cognitive dissonance is at work. If you did awaken bright and early, and got right to work producing a realistic budget, you would have proven your earlier self-assessment wrong. Your mind doesn't like you to be wrong, so it goes to work proving you were right all along.

When you tell yourself,

"I will wake up refreshed, an hour ahead of schedule, and use that quiet time to start setting up a realistic family budget," your mind, again, sets out to prove you are right.

When you eliminate "impossibility thinking," you open doors to achieving goals you never thought possible. Let your mind get busy proving you're right about what you decide is possible, instead of setting about to validate your assessment of what you've deemed impossible.

QUICK REFERENCE

What you can do right now:
Banish the word "impossible" from your vocabulary. Substitute a more accurate and positive phrase to describe what appears infeasible.

Instead of saying,

"I realize that you want to earn enough money to buy yourself a car this summer, but it's impossible. Insurance costs for you would be outrageous."

Say,

"I know you'd like to have your own car, and it will take a lot of money to buy one and then make sure you have adequate insurance coverage. Let's work on a re-

alistic plan and discuss it with your father tonight. If this summer doesn't seem realistic, let's see about aiming for Christmas."

Instead of saying,

"Get promoted to Account Executive before the end of the year? That's impossible! I'd need at least twelve months of experience and there are already two other Sales Assistants in line for the next opening."

Say,

"As far as I know, nobody has yet been promoted to Account Executive in under a year. I want to be the first. I'm going to work as hard as I can to build a really outstanding performance record."

Instead of saying,

"This is impossible."

Say,

"This is going to require some special effort, and it can be done."

11. Kids Are All Ears

Your hefty teenager joins in with some younger children down the street as they play on a slip-'n'-slide toy stretched across their front lawn. When your large boy runs and slides down the vinyl runway, his mass and momentum combine and he shoots past the end of the strip, wrecking the plastic pool, leveling the neighbor's gladiolus, and snapping off one of the automatic sprinkler system's riser pipes.

Say out loud to yourself:

"John! What's the matter with you? Now look what you've done, you stupid kid. You've wrecked the Tates' front yard. You never act your age. You're going to get in trouble all your life, aren't you?"

Now, say:

"John! Looks like you're going to be doing some gardening. I know you mean well, and you're getting too big to play with young children's yard toys."

Which sounds like a parent who'll encourage his child to use good judgment and grow gracefully into young adulthood? Which will steer his child to a future of self-esteem problems?

When little Julie was only six years old, she had a very short attention span. She had little interest in school and failed third grade. By the fourth grade, her performance had improved very little, so her teacher conferred with her understandably concerned parents. She informed them, "You might as well face it, Julie will never be any more than an average student."

It's amazing how perceptive young children are. Although Julie doesn't remember her teacher ever directly telling her of her discouraging assessment, she somehow got the message.

Julie performed at an average level all through elementary and junior high school. Always insecure about her mediocre scholastic performance, she formed most of her friendships with people who didn't excel in much of anything. They expected little of her, and that's what she delivered.

In ninth grade, Julie contracted mononucleosis and stayed home in bed for nine weeks. With few distractions, she threw herself into catching up on the schoolwork that she was missing by being out of class. For the first time she discovered that with some hard work she could be an A student and not an average one.

Twenty years later, a veterinarian noticed how Julie, at age 33, loved caring for horses. He told her she had a gift for diagnosing diseases and encouraged her to go to college, saying she was too smart not to. For some reason she believed him. Enrolled in some of the nearby college classes (and no longer burdened by the belief that she is destined to be "nothing more than average"), she's doing much better. Her G.P.A. is 3.82!

Julie had an unusual last name that you may have heard before: Ziglar. Her father is Zig Ziglar, one of the best-known professional sales trainers and speakers in the world. I first heard Julie Ziglar Norman's story over lunch with Zig and his wife, Jean. My wife and I had our then 3-month-old baby, Kelcie, with us and I asked Zig for some advice about what messages we should be giving our little girl every day during her most formative stage of life. Zig is the author of *Raising Positive Kids in a Negative World*, an outstanding book that every parent should read. In it, Zig cites an anonymous quotation:

> *Your Home Is Bugged!*
> *In every home there are two microphones per child—one in each ear. These highly sensitive instruments pick up the table prayers, the songs sung, ordinary conversation, and all types of language. These all-hearing microphones transmit all they hear to highly impressionable minds. These sounds then become the vocabulary of the child and the basis for action.*

I know from personal experience that children are highly susceptible to negative messages. I was told I had Dumbo ears as a kid, and even though the rest of my body eventually caught up, I saw myself as an ugly person right up until my late 20s. Whenever I looked in a mirror, it was as if the image was peculiarly distorted—like a weird fun-house mirror with two convex bulges—all I could see were those two huge, unbecoming ears.

What you say, and what others say, has a very powerful influence on your child's self-image. A bruised self-image will take years to heal, if it ever does.

Dr. Wayne Dyer, in his wonderful book *What Do You Really Want for Your Children?*, reminds all parents that they may be inadvertently lowering their children's self-confidence and self-worth. One common mistake is to tell kids that they are bad children, when the truth is that they are good children behaving badly. It may sound like there's not much difference between:

> "You bad girl! You ruined the wallpaper when you drew on it with those crayons. Why are you so destructive?"

and,

> "Drawing on the walls is bad. Now you've ruined our wallpaper. That was very destructive."

While there is a huge difference in the psychological effects those two admonitions create, children are not yet able to grasp such subtle distinctions. We adults must take responsibility for making our approval of the child, and disapproval of the action, ultraclear.

Kids also shape their futures with their own language. When you hear your child say,

> "I always goof up my arithmetic. I'm dumb with numbers. I don't want to take the test. I have a tummyache."

nip that powerless language in the bud:

> **"Jenny, you're very good with numbers. You're quite smart at figuring out how much change you should get when I give you a dollar to buy some fruit. You can do**

super well on the arithmetic quiz. Let's practice together right now."

I take Zig Ziglar's and Wayne Dyer's advice seriously. Though my little Kelcie doesn't talk yet, I'm sure she understands my feelings, if not my words. I will never let a half a day pass without reminding her that she is a good, smart, beautiful person with a wonderful and rewarding life ahead of her.

Teaching your children to be Power Talkers is one of the most wonderful gifts you can give. Show them by your own example that you project positive expectations, for them and for yourself. And keep in mind that any children you interact with, whether they're relatives, neighbors, or kids you talk with for a few minutes while standing in line at the supermarket or sitting on an airplane, are weighing every word you say. We reap what we sow.

QUICK REFERENCE

What you can do right now:
Be especially conscious of Power Talking whenever you are around youngsters. Set an example and help shape kids' futures by speaking positively to and about them.

Instead of saying,

"You bad boy! You knocked over Mommy's vase and broke it."

Say,

"When you run in the house, it's easy to accidentally break things. Please don't. Keep on being such a good runner and always run outside."

Instead of saying,

"Oh, kids, I'm sorry we can't go to Disneyland, but we

can't afford it. Daddy's not very good at keeping jobs, so he got fired again."

Say,

"Kids, we're going to shift our plans and go to Disneyland next year, when you're a little bigger and you can go on more of the rides. Daddy's going to make an exciting change and get a new job he'll like better than his old one. We're going to save up the money and really look forward to an even better vacation."

Instead of saying,

"You're a bad child and you're always getting into trouble."

Say,

"You're a good child, and that behavior is not acceptable."

II. Give Credit Where Due

Power Talkers give credit wherever credit is due. They don't hesitate to applaud others when they succeed, and they also give themselves credit whenever they create positive events in their own lives.

The effect your manner of speaking can have on your life has been carefully researched, and the results are dramatic. Dr. Martin Seligman, a psychologist at the University of Pennsylvania, has done outstanding work on the subject. The results of his research are reported in his book, *Learned Optimism*.

Dr. Seligman identified three main scales of optimism and pessimism in a person's common daily language, or "explanatory style." When faced with positive events, optimistic Power Talkers describe them using "universal," "internal," and "permanent" terms. Powerless pessimists tend to attribute positive events to "specific," "external," and "temporary" factors.

"Universal" means that you notice your success not just in one particular instance, but in all aspects of your life. "Specific" explanations mean that you see positive situations as isolated events.

"Internal" terms connote that you take personal responsibility, that you recognize your own role in bringing about positive outcomes, and give yourself credit for it. An "external" explanatory style means that you attribute the success to something beyond your control—to "a lucky break."

"Permanent" descriptions identify positive events as continuing evidence of your regular pattern of success. A "temporary" description says it's a fluke, a once-in-a-while happening.

When a Power Talking mother sees her son hit a home run that helps his Little League team win their game, she later tells him,

> "I'm so proud of you, son. You really did a great job, and all that batting practice is really paying off. You hit well in the last game, too, and I'll bet you'll do even better during the playoffs. Your schoolwork is improving, you've been getting your chores done on time, and you've cut way down on junk food. I'd say you're hitting all kinds of home runs."

You can easily detect her universal, internal, permanent explanation.

A mom who's not tuned in to the importance of what she says to her children might say:

> "You sure got lucky that time. That pitcher gave you a ball that only a farm leaguer could miss. And it's a good thing the wind was blowing out toward left field. Too bad you don't hit like that more often. You'd better enjoy the glory while you can. You've got that science test tomorrow, and you know it's your worst subject."

The powerless parent uses a specific, external, temporary description for the same event. The home run is an isolated event, due to external factors, and certainly not something that will continue. Which parent do you suppose has the more successful, happy child?

In business, the most effective leaders are those who publicly credit members of their teams when they succeed. If you want to develop loyal workers who keep on getting better and better, make sure you give them credit for their accomplishments. The same is true in personal relationships—great friendships are built on mutual admiration. Think about how much it means to you when someone you respect, trust, and perhaps love gives you heartfelt recognition for your personal accomplishments.

In the chapters ahead, you'll meet people who benefit from taking credit for their own accomplishments. You'll also see the beneficial results of acknowledging the credit others deserve for their achievements. Be a Power Talker; give credit wherever it's due.

12. What's Your Excuse?

You offer your colleague a ride home and when you get to her house, she invites you in for a cup of coffee.

She says:

"Oh, you'll have to excuse the mess. I left in a hurry this morning and the place looks terrible."

Or she says:

"Welcome to my home."

Whose home will appear neater to you? Where will you feel more comfortable? Who sounds like the more confident, secure person?

What a good hypnotist can do with a group of otherwise

serious, reserved business executives attending their company's annual banquet is utterly amazing—and hilarious. Gil Eagles is one of the world's finest. He's hired by IBM, AT&T, and other top corporations when they want a world-class performance for their most important events. He can bring a group of corporate leaders up onstage, and within a few minutes, have them impersonating Elvis, reeling in fighting marlins, or behaving like demanding drill sergeants. Sitting in the audience, you just can't believe it when you see good old Joe, the mild-mannered, rather shy Senior Accountant you've known for years, up there wildly clicking imaginary castanets and performing a spirited flamenco dance in front of a thousand employees who've hardly ever heard him make a peep.

Gil is quick to debunk the misconceptions popularized by old-school hypnotists: He does not put his subjects into a trance or induce a state of suspended consciousness. What any hypnotist really does is help his subjects create and live out a mental image.

If he suggests that they'll be embarrassed and look like fools, they won't cooperate. Instead, Gil brings his group of volunteers up onstage and paints an elaborate and reassuring mental picture so they can see themselves succeeding. As they sit—eyes closed—in a row of chairs facing the audience, he tells them that they'll feel **relaxed** and emphasizes that the whole purpose is **entertainment.** He says, "*You* will be the **stars**, and I will get to share in the credit." He asks the watching audience to "Give these **brave** people a round of applause."

With these statements, Gil creates a mental picture in his subjects' minds: They will be relaxed, brave, and entertaining star performers. Then he helps them act out those images.

Gil's success as a hypnotist is founded on one basic premise: People act out the pictures in their head. After more than 4000 masterful performances, he's very conscious of the images he creates onstage. Offstage, we all unconsciously project images we really don't intend. Gil and I both learned something about creating unintended pictures when I visited with him and his family.

After giving a speech in New York City, I called Gil and he offered to pick me up in Manhattan and drive me out to his home in New Jersey. From there, we'd head north to relax with his family at their weekend home in the Poconos. "All right, I'll pick you up at 1:00 in front of the hotel. You'll have to excuse my car, it's an old battered-up Cadillac."

Sure enough, he pulled up at the hotel in a marvelous classic Caddy and we drove to his home in Short Hills, N.J. His is a very exclusive, affluent community of corporate executives, doctors, and lawyers. Many of the residences are million-dollar mansions. As we walked into Gil's large, beautiful, antique-filled home, he said, "You'll have to excuse the mess; the dog has absolutely devastated the whole downstairs."

Soon we were all seated in the roomy Cadillac, cruising north through Pennsylvania to enjoy a weekend at the Eagles' lakefront cottage. As we pulled into the driveway, dozens of deer grazed along the roadside, the view over the small lake was serene, and their lovely house on the shore looked very inviting. Gil's welcoming comment was, "You'll have to excuse our little shack."

I've never enjoyed a more relaxing, comfortable weekend, or appreciated better friendships. There was absolutely no need for Gil to offer any excuses for anything. His home, car, and cottage were all delightful.

Unintentionally, though, Gil had "programmed" me to notice the slightly worn leather upholstery in his car and the teethmarks his magnificent Husky had left on the sofa's legs.

When I called it to his attention later, Gil couldn't believe he'd created those images. He's tremendously successful and is anything but insecure, yet he had unconsciously painted mental pictures that could make him appear ashamed of his home and car and cottage.

The whole point of Power Talking is this: The first step in using more powerful language is to become conscious of your negative habits so that you catch yourself right after using a powerless phrase. Then, you learn to catch yourself just *before* using the powerless version, and make the Power Talking substitution. And finally, you develop the unconscious habit of speaking powerfully all the time.

If you're ever fortunate enough to visit Gil, I expect you'll now hear him saying, "You can't miss me, I'll be driving a classic white Cadillac. You'll feel completely at home with my family. We're not stuffy or pretentious, as you'll see when you notice how comfortable our dog feels gnawing on the furniture. And you'll love our cozy cottage in the Poconos."

When I'm onstage delivering a Power Talking seminar, I often catch myself letting a powerless phrase slip out. I may say "but" rather than "and," or "I'll have to check on that," rather than "I'll be glad to check on that." To my live audience, and to you, my reader, I emphasize the critical point: Power Talking isn't a destination, it's a journey. Every day, I'm aware of my language and working to improve it. You can do the same.

When you say, "You'll have to excuse my . . . house/car/ cooking/performance," your apology has two effects: First, you call attention to a condition **you're** uncomfortable about—and the other person may not otherwise have noticed. Second, you make yourself appear insecure.

Have you noticed that people who offer excuses rarely need to? As soon as they say, "You'll have to excuse my messy house," you're probably thinking, "What's she apologizing for? It's a lot neater than mine." Or, "She's right. Now that I'm scrutinizing, I can see that those knick-knacks need a good dusting."

If people are going to be offended by the appearance of

your home, or messy office, or dirty car, let them. It's their loss. In reality, most won't notice what you're uncomfortable about—if you don't call attention to it. And those who do shouldn't concern you. Now, if you've invited your boss to dinner and are genuinely concerned that your tiny apartment or orange-crate furnishings will make a negative impression, meet at an appropriate restaurant instead.

In short, don't apologize for something you feel insecure about. Fix it or forget it. Given the choice of meeting someone who's insecure and uncomfortable—with good reason or not—and someone who seems content and happy, I'd much rather be around the relaxed person.

QUICK REFERENCE

What you can do right now:
Stop making excuses and apologizing for some imagined shortcoming. Either change it or forget it.

Instead of saying,

"You'll have to excuse my messy apartment. I just haven't had time to clean it up this week."

Say,

"Welcome. I'm glad to see you."

Instead of saying,

"Please pardon the piles of junk in my office. I've been so busy lately, I'm afraid it looks like a shambles!"

Say,

"Come into my office, I'll move some of these things out of your way."

Instead of saying,

"We could take my car if you can put up with the old clunker. I'm planning to get a new one, and meanwhile this one's going downhill fast."

Say,

"Let's take my car."

Instead of saying,

"You'll have to excuse my car/mess/hair/house."

Say,

Nothing!

13. It's Just My Opinion

The executive whose phone you're answering is unavailable, and the caller asks when he should call back.
Say out loud to yourself:

"I'm afraid I wouldn't know that, I'm just a receptionist. I could be wrong, but maybe in the morning. That's only my guess, I really can't say for sure."

Now, say:

"My name's Bob Wilkins, and I'm the receptionist. Please tell me a little about your call, and I'll confirm when she'll be available to talk with you."

Which sounds like someone who's proud of his work?

Who has low self-esteem, represents his boss poorly, and is unlikely to go very far in his career?

One of my clients asked me to participate in panel interviews of two finalist candidates being considered for a senior management position. Both possessed superb technical skills for the job; each had demonstrated an excellent ability to lead a department similar to that he or she would manage if chosen to fill this position.

While other interview panelists asked specific questions about the candidates' experiences and career accomplishments, I concentrated my attention on how each one spoke.

The first candidate began by saying:

"I'm Gwen Moss, and I'm here to present myself to you as a candidate to manage your Call Center. Two days ago, I received my packet of background materials and the set of six formal questions you're asking each candidate. I'll begin this morning by answering each of them for you."

The second began by saying:

"I'm Brian Bayer. Unfortunately, I only got your information and questions a couple of days ago, so I must confess that I haven't really had much of a chance to go through them in detail. I've taken a guess at some of the numbers and what I think you want to know. I could be way off, but after all, it's just my opinion."

One of the formal questions asked the candidates to "Please describe your philosophy regarding Customer Service processes from each of several perspectives." This question was broken down into important areas including hiring staff, training them, measuring quality vs. productivity, and so on.

The first candidate said,

"I firmly believe that . . ."

and she went on to explain some of her beliefs about Customer Service, including:

"Front-line employees must be empowered to solve, not pass the buck."
"If you're in doubt—DON'T HIRE!"
"If you're not moving ahead, you're falling behind."

The second said,

"I made up a little handout for you on my home computer. You'll have to excuse me, but I couldn't do it on a more powerful machine with a laser printer, so it doesn't look too good. Unfortunately, I only have access to an old dot matrix printer. As you'll see, I included some of the things I like to say about Customer Service. They're just some of my little slogans."

And they were listed in his handout:

"Service should be worth waiting for."
"Motivate employees to welcome difficult callers."
"Marketing is a philosophy, not a department."

As the hour-long panel discussion concluded, each candidate was given a few minutes to summarize.
Gwen said:

"I feel ideally suited to manage this department, and I want to work with you. In the words of your CEO, which I read in your most recent annual report, 'I can't think of a more exciting place to work.' I can see why he said that. This is where I want to be. Thank you for your consideration."

Brian said:

"Well, I don't really have much to add at this point. It's pretty much up to you, now. I'm sure I'm just one of the people you're considering. I saw where your CEO said, 'I can't think of a more exciting place to work.' I thought that was kinda neat, and I'm only hoping I'll get the opportunity to work here."

Aside from the candidates' phrasing, they were a toss-up. Both had very strong skills, backgrounds, and technical competence.

The dramatic differences in their levels of self-esteem were evident in their speaking styles. The first candidate confidently presented her answers to each question. The second (who'd had the same amount of preparation time) apologized for not having had enough time to prepare more thoroughly. The first stated her analyses with conviction; the second excused his by characterizing them as "only my opinion."

When it was time to summarize, the first postured herself as the ideal choice, though she did not arrogantly proclaim herself a shoo-in. The second lowered himself to "just one of the people you're considering" when in fact he was one of the two finalists.

The substance of what each said carried equal value. Their styles of saying it were polar opposites. Consider their two lists of Customer Service philosophies, for example. They could easily have been swapped; both made sense and summarized important principles. Prefacing Gwen's list with an "I firmly believe" statement added importance to them. Prefacing Brian's with the denigrating phrase, "They're just some of my little slogans," devalued them.

My recommendation was to hire the first qualified candidate. What's yours?

Kay White is responsible for Pacific Bell's telemarketing training throughout California. She believes that our words reveal how we really feel about ourselves. They serve as a barometer that indicates our self-esteem levels. A poor self-image becomes a self-fulfilling prophecy. She says, "How you're treated depends on the way you behave. If you say you're 'only' a Customer Associate, you're saying you don't think much of your position, and customers treat you as someone with little authority."

Kay teaches her trainees to avoid belittling language. The Customer Associates listen to each others' self-descriptive language and tell each other if they hear diminishing terms. Her "nickel-in-the-jar" technique is particularly effective. Rather than just keeping a stroke tally of their verbal slips, trainees actually deposit five cents in the kitty each time they put themselves down. Each "plink" reminds them to think about the value of self-supporting language.

Kay also recognizes that her middle managers play an important role. They help shape an employee's self-image with every comment they make. She seeks to rid managers of such comments as,

"Considering your performance last month, I'm not at all surprised that you failed to reach quota this month. I just never can count on you, can I?"

You may react to those phrases by saying, "But what manager would ever be so stupid (and cruel) as to say things like that?" Well, plenty do. Maybe you've worked for one.

One of Kay White's important goals is to show her managers how to commend and reprimand employees. When someone performs well, she reminds managers to avoid personality-oriented praise, and instead offer specific behavior-oriented compliments.

Rather than saying:

"You're really an asset to my department. You're delightful and I'm pleased to have you here."

say specifically what you notice:

"Jolene, you did an excellent job of handling that customer's question. Your answer was perfectly accurate,

and you also provided it in a friendly, caring way. Your word choice and tone of voice were both very support- ive. I really appreciate your good work."

Kay reminds her managers that such praise must always be sincere and honest. If it's not, the listener's red flag raises and he discounts what he hears, thinking to himself:

"I can tell when someone's trying to manipulate me. I can figure out what you **really** think of me."

Of course, the result of insincere praise would be a counter-productive undermining of the employee's self- image. This low self-esteem then leaks out whenever the employee talks with customers.

When it's necessary to reprimand an employee, a manag- er's goal should be to change an unacceptable behavior, not diminish the person's self-image. Kay recommends using the "Criticism Sandwich" technique. Sandwich the negative information between two positive messages:

"Terry, you've really been improving with your cus- tomer contacts. For example, your answer to that last caller's question was completely accurate. Your tone of voice could have been friendlier, and I'd like you to work on that in the next call. Keep up the good work with your accuracy. I can see that you've really mas- tered the technical material from your training course."

Whether talking to yourself, describing your accomplish- ments, or commenting on another person's performance, avoid diminishing language.

QUICK REFERENCE

What you can do right now:
You're not "just" or "only" anything. Describe yourself, your beliefs, and your accomplishments positively and proudly.

Instead of saying,

"I've just been here for a few months, but the way I see things . . ."

Say,

"I've been carefully observing for the last few months, and the way I see things . . ."

Instead of saying,

"Well, it's only my opinion, of course, and I could be wrong about this, but I would say . . ."

Say,

"I believe . . ."

Instead of saying,

"I'm just the receptionist, so I probably wouldn't be able to help you very much."

Say,

"I'm the receptionist and I'll be happy to help you."

Instead of saying,

"I'm only just the . . ."

Say,

"I am the . . ."

14. Is "Luck" Getting the Credit for Your Hard Work?

A project you spearheaded has just received significant recognition at your firm's parent company. Your boss tells you that you're being talked about at headquarters as an up-and-comer. He asks, "How did you do it?"

Say out loud to yourself:

"Well, I'm not really sure. I guess I just got lucky. I've handled dozens of projects like that one and I guess someone just happened to notice this one."

Now, say:

"I worked hard! On that particular project, I incorporated the feedback I've received from the last several reports, and I'm pleased to see it really hit the target. I have an excellent support staff and they contributed a great deal, too."

Which sounds like the employee with the brighter future? Whose good work is likely to be repeated on the next big project?

If you don't have a strong relationship with a personal physician, and you suddenly need a doctor, where do you turn? You can contact a referral service such as the successful Ask-A-Nurse program, available to nearly half of the U.S. population. You can phone Ask-A-Nurse 24 hours a day, free of charge.

You wake up at 3:00 one morning with a throbbing left foot. Nothing shows—there are no cuts or bruises—but it hurts so much you can hardly get out of bed. Should you try to sleep and then limp in to work and see if it feels better later? Soak it in warm water? Should you see a doctor? What could it be?

A call to Ask-A-Nurse puts you in touch with a friendly, professional Registered Nurse who asks you about your symptoms. She uses a computer program that prompts her to ask the appropriate questions, and follows strict medical protocol. As you answer, it becomes clear to her that you should have the condition investigated further, right away.

The nurse directs you to a nearby hospital's emergency room, provides driving directions, and alerts them to expect you. After the visit she calls you back to check up and ensure that you were well cared for at the hospital. If you need to see an orthopedic physician, or another specialist, she'll recommend one that's convenient and meets your criteria. Of course, if all you need is an aspirin and an Ace bandage until you can contact your own physician, she'll say so during your initial call.

The Ask-A-Nurse program is a terrific hospital marketing and public relations tool. Not only does it bring in new patients, it also forms the basis for a long-term relationship between the hospital and the patient. The program is also a tremendous benefit to the community. Without charge, anyone can receive a Registered Nurse's confidential, professional assessment. (Only physicians provide diagnoses.)

As you can imagine, the success of this program rests squarely on the shoulders—or voice, actually—of the nurse who answers your call. Is she technically competent? Does she ask the right questions? Is she pleasant and understanding? Does she give the right answers? If she sounds vague or wishy-washy, or seems unsure of her assessment, you're not likely to trust or follow her advice.

Hospitals that offer the Ask-A-Nurse program in their communities are very particular about whom they hire. Interviews are extensive, and begin with a telephone screening. After all, if the nurse can't handle a pressured situation like a job interview over the phone, how will she do when a frantic mother calls to explain that her child faces a serious medical emergency?

When the program manager asks an applicant about her strengths and weaknesses, she'd better not hem and haw. Wrong answer:

> "Oh well, I'm not really sure what I'd say my strongest points are. I guess, uh, well, it's hard to say. I was pretty lucky when I got a job at Bellevue in New York City. You get everything thrown at you there, you know. So I guess you could say I've been involved in a pretty wide range of situations."

Right answer,

> **"My two greatest strengths are what make me feel confident about pursuing this opportunity with you. First, I really enjoy relating to people in need. That's why I entered nursing in the first place. Being able to talk with and help 30 to 50 patients on the phone each day, compared with 15 or 25 on the floor, is appealing. Second, I have experience in a wide range of medical situations. Early in my career I set my sights on the most diversified institution I could find, and that was Bellevue Hospital in Manhattan. We built an outstanding nursing program there, and I'm pleased to have played a major role in reorganizing the department."**

In the words of Pat Stricker, Ask-A-Nurse Program Manager at The Toledo Hospital in Ohio,

> *"I like it when people aren't afraid to tell me what they're good at. If they say, 'Well, gee, I don't know,' they probably lack the self-confidence we're looking for. On the other hand, if they're egotistical or boastful, I know they won't fit in well with the team."*

Life is like one long series of interviews. People are sizing you up constantly—before you're hired, when you're considered for promotions, at significant milestones, and during normal daily conversations. When you deserve credit, give it to yourself. People whose opinions can help you succeed want to believe in people who already believe in themselves.

There are two big reasons for giving yourself credit whenever you're proud of your own accomplishments: (1) Others respect you for it, and (2) You deserve and benefit from it.

Don't write off your accomplishments as "lucky." People don't respect that kind of response. What you really should say is,

> **"Thank you. I worked hard and I'm very grateful for this recognition. My support team helped a great deal, too."**

The way you react to praise helps others size you up as one who is either boastful, falsely modest, or appropriately appreciative.

The second reason for accepting credit when you deserve it is even more important. We all respond to rewards, and those that carry the most weight may be the rewards we give ourselves. When you say to yourself,

> **"I feel so good about winning this award. I worked hard and this makes it worthwhile,"**

you've reinforced your own successful behavior.

In other words, giving yourself credit results in immediate and satisfying ego gratification, and it also promotes repeat performances.

When screening candidates during job interviews, I've noticed that their overuse of "I" phrases is a real turnoff. When a candidate says,

> **"I accomplished this and that, I won such-and-such an award, I turned our department around, I brought about a 22% revenue increase . . ."**

the interviewer may feel cautious about this person's ability to work well with a team, and may also question the individual's professed 100% responsibility for departmental achievements. It's much more effective to share in the credit without hogging it all for yourself:

"Our department made some very significant improvements during my leadership. Together we generated a 22% revenue increase, and as a result I was awarded the Manager of the Year plaque. It feels great!"

Take credit for your accomplishments. When others ask, let them know—modestly—that your success is a direct result of your diligent work plus the support of the others who helped. And when you talk to yourself, be sure that you reward and reinforce your own role in creating your success.

QUICK REFERENCE

What you can do right now:
When you succeed, modestly, acknowledge your own role in attaining your accomplishments, both to yourself and to others.

Instead of saying to yourself,

"Gee, I can't understand why they picked me for this award. I haven't really done anything special to deserve it. I just got lucky."

Say,

"I don't always give myself enough credit. This award is proof that my talents and hard work are appreciated by others. It's time I recognized more of my own accomplishments."

Instead of saying,

"A lot of things just kind of went my way. I was lucky enough to guess right on the forecast for next year, and, what do you know, it just all came out pretty much like management was hoping it would."

Say,

"I drew on my past experience to forecast for next year, and incorporating management's views, the results were very accurate."

Instead of saying,

"I got lucky."

Say,

"I planned well and worked hard."

15. What They Don't Know Won't Hurt Them

While visiting friends, someone suggests that you play bridge. Mary asks if you'll be her partner.

Say out loud to yourself:

"Well, I'll be your partner, all right, but I'm really not too good at cards. You'll have to forgive me if I make some stupid mistakes. I hope I don't make us lose."

Now, say:

"Great, let's play."

Which sounds like Mary will regret having asked you to play with her? Which leaves the door open for a fun, challenging game?

There are so many instances where people "cover themselves" by building a safety net of excuses, anticipating that they'll fail. Chances are if you say nothing people won't realize you're insecure about your abilities. The only person being supercritical of your performance is . . . you.

Last summer I set a personal goal of joining in on three open beach volleyball games. That may not seem like much of a goal to you, but for me it was an important accomplishment. I wasn't very athletic as a boy. I didn't voluntarily join in any athletic events, and in high school was able to secure my letter in sports only by serving as manager of the gymnastics team. As a result, I've felt insecure about participating in sports.

Still, there's no good reason why I couldn't be a fine athlete. I'm tall, well-proportioned, and have good coordination. My only shortcoming has been my attitude of athletic insecurity.

Sure enough, I did achieve my modest goal and joined in those three volleyball games. I enjoyed them thoroughly and played creditably. During the third game a brother and sister approached and asked if they could play. The sister, Stacy, a young woman about 25 years old, joined our team. She walked onto the court and said, "Gee, are you sure you guys want to have me on your team?" Sure enough, she did miss most balls coming toward her, but her lack of skill was exceeded by her lack of self-esteem. Every time she missed the ball, she'd say, "Oh, I'm sorry, I'm so bad at this. If you want me off the team just say so." It became embarrassing to play with her because all of us could just imagine what torment she was feeling, knowing that she'd probably flub the next volley.

Soon it was her turn to serve. She immediately prepared

us all by saying, "This is going to be terrible. I can never even get the ball over the net." And of course she didn't. It was obvious that no one had ever shown Stacy how to serve, so I called for a time-out and gave her a quick lesson. The other team, being good sports, gave her another chance. On her next try, Stacy made an excellent serve which the opposing team did not return. Twice more she served very well, gaining points each time.

I could identify with Stacy because I know that of all the few times I've been coerced into some kind of athletic encounter, I've begun by apologizing for my expected poor performance and repeatedly beaten myself up for playing without skill. Stacy would have been much better off—as would I—had we simply played our best. Nobody in our volleyball game was an expert player, and her lack of skill would have been hardly noticed had she not called attention to her own ineptitude. Her performance would have been much better if instead of deriding her own serving ability she had simply said, "Would one of you show me how to hold the ball when I serve? It's been a while."

Do your best without telling people that you think your best isn't very good.

QUICK REFERENCE

What you can do right now:
You're probably far more critical of yourself than anybody else will be. Go ahead and enjoy doing as well as you can.

Instead of saying,

"Well, I'm certainly no artist, but I'll try to sketch out a drawing of how this new process would work. I hope you'll be able to figure out what I mean despite all this horrible scribbling."

Say,

"I'll diagram this new process to make it clearer."

Instead of saying,

"I'm just terrible in the kitchen, but, well, I gave it a shot. I tried to make Fettucine Alfredo. I hope you can gag it down without getting too sick."

Say,

"I hope you'll enjoy eating my Fettucine Alfredo as much as I enjoyed preparing it for you."

Instead of saying,

"I'm really not too good at this."

Proceed to do your best without excuses.

16. Ken and Spencer Were Right!

You're talking with a peer about your department's tidy appearance. He comments that your area always appears well looked after—much neater than his own.

Say out loud to yourself:

"Well, that's the way I like it. I'm always telling the admin people around here that I expect this place to look shipshape. They do pretty well. They'd better."

Now, say:

"You know, you're right. My people really are good about keeping this area looking sharp. Mind if I tell them you said so? I'd like to let 'em know that I'm not the only one who notices and appreciates their good work."

Which sounds like the manager whose people will continue keeping the area neat and putting in a little extra effort? Which one probably has a morale problem, high turnover, and people who don't really enjoy working with him?

While vacationing with my family, I had my only first-hand encounter with a professional wrestler. Hawk, a member of the Road Warriors professional wrestling team, stayed in the condo development we were visiting. Within hours of his arrival at the resort, every kid and most of the adults staying in the complex knew he was there. He was immense and muscular and certainly caught everyone's attention the first time he stretched out to lounge beside the pool in his leopard-patterned swim shorts.

After observing a steady stream of autograph seekers and picture takers approach him by the pool, I settled into a lounge chair beside Hawk's and began to read. I probably wouldn't have chosen to stake my claim so close to him, but it was one of the few vacant chairs available. There was a kind of "clear zone" around Hawk. I guess most people felt as self-conscious as I did about sitting there and attempting not to stare.

It was impossible to ignore his conversations, considering his very loud, gravelly voice. It was understandable that very few adults approached Hawk to talk, because he certainly had an imposing physical appearance. Many children, however, walked right up to him and conversed quite comfortably. Most were young boys, and I imagined that many had probably said to their parents, "Someday I want to be a big, strong muscleman like him."

I was surprised to hear how Hawk talked with these children. He spoke in entirely positive terms. He didn't tell the boys, "You're a little pipsqueak, but if you work really hard, maybe someday you can be big and strong like me." Instead he told them that they were already growing strong. Even when skinny, underdeveloped kids came up to ask for his autograph, he'd find something positive and complimentary to say. "Your arms are really long. I'll bet you're a terrific basketball player."

After overhearing many such conversations, I got up the nerve to start talking with him myself. I told Hawk how impressed I had been with the way he handled kids, and it was then that I realized he was doing so totally by design. He said, "It's such an easy thing to do, and it can make such a big difference to these little guys." Not only was there a heck of a nice person underneath all the flesh and muscle, he was consciously guiding those kids to think highly of themselves.

Hawk was genuinely moved when I complimented him on his positive behavior with the kids. I'm sure that he hears no end of praise and admiration for his physique, but I suspect that very few people stop to tell Hawk they admire anything deeper than his physical appearance.

That conversation with Hawk completely changed my uneducated view of professional wrestlers. I've never before intentionally watched a professional wrestling match on television. If all those other big lugs are as sensitive, caring, and positive as Hawk, I may become a fan.

Ken Blanchard and Spencer Johnson were right! When they took the business book market by storm with *One Minute Manager* and its many spin-off books, they advocated "Catching People Doing Things Right." They correctly asserted that this was one of the most underused and most effective management tools around.

Power Talkers give credit wherever it's due, especially

when it's unexpected. This whole book emphasizes two major audiences for your language: you, and the other people who hear you. Everyone benefits when you give credit to others for their accomplishments, even when it's just something little.

I live in a lovely wooded neighborhood near Seattle. The approach to my street is a long, steep hill with a center planting strip that extends for nearly a quarter of a mile. Throughout the year, the plants are trimmed, pruned, and rotated. After the azaleas' brief glory of intense, fiery red blossoms, somebody plants pansies in great numbers. When they wither, marigolds and lobelia appear. Somebody goes to a lot of trouble keeping that planting strip looking good. It's not automatic. The "somebody" is Susan. Every now and then I've noticed this woman digging and clipping and pruning and planting.

I'm sure most of my neighbors have commented to themselves about how beautiful and well-tended that strip is. One day I thought it was about time Susan found out how much her work is appreciated. I pulled over to the curb as I drove down the hill, lowered my window, and said,

"You do very nice work. I see you out here often, making sure the plants look good. Your efforts really pay off; they always look great. Thank you for being so conscientious about your work. I enjoy seeing it every time I drive up or down the hill."

Her face blossomed as beautifully as any of the annuals she had been planting. With a big smile, she said,

"I'm really glad you enjoy my work. I like doing it, too. Thank you for stopping. It makes me feel really good to know that you notice."

She's not the only one who felt good. Offering someone a compliment can make the complimenter feel just about as good as the one who's complimented. With Susan the gardener, that moment of seeing her smile and feel appreciated was well worth pulling over for. And, what's more, I feel extra good every time I drive by her handiwork, knowing that she probably thinks about my comment from time to time. When I see another round of fresh flowers coming into bloom, I know I haven't taken them or her for granted.

Since much of my speaking and consulting work is dedicated to fostering professionalism on the telephone, I'm especially attentive to people who do a great job handling my phone calls. When a secretary answers the phone in a clear, friendly manner, I take a moment to comment. When a Customer Service representative deals with my question professionally, I let that person know he did a good job. I especially enjoy complimenting telephone operators who handle my calls well. Hotel operators, in particular, seem shocked that a guest would take an extra moment to offer a commendation. I end up feeling just as good as they do.

Invest a moment, every day, to "catch people doing things right," as Ken and Spencer suggested. Tell them what you notice and why you appreciate it. You'll both feel great about it.

QUICK REFERENCE

What you can do right now:
Go out of your way to compliment people and give them credit for doing things right, especially when they don't expect it.

Instead of saying to yourself,

"Someone sure does a nice job with the lettering on those signs at the drugstore. It must be someone who studied calligraphy."

Say to the store manager,

"Who makes those signs I see all over your store? They do a darn good job, and I'd like to tell 'em so, myself."

Instead of saying,

"Her kids sure are quiet and well-behaved."

Say,

"You've obviously given your children a lot of positive attention. They interact with everyone so politely and intelligently."

Instead of saying,

"That daughter of mine is a big help around the house."

Say,

"Darling, you are a big help around the house, and I appreciate it."

17. You're About as Old as You Say You Are

Your grown children invite you to join them for their annual trip to the family's country cabin.

Say out loud to yourself:

"I'm not a kid anymore, you know. I'm too old to enjoy that kind of thing."

Now, say:

"That'll be fun. I'd enjoy a change of scene, and of course, I like to be with you."

Which sounds like someone who'll live out his years in happiness, surrounded by people who enjoy his company? Which is likely to become a bitter, depressed, lonely old man his children won't really want to visit?

An audience member asked Dr. Norman Vincent Peale, author of *The Power of Positive Thinking*, why, at age 92, he continued to give speeches rather than quietly retiring to enjoy the life he'd made for himself.

"Why? . . . I'll . . . tell you . . . why. Because, . . . despite all the speeches . . . I've given . . . over the years . . . and despite . . . the many books, . . . there are still a few negative thinkers out there!"

The audience rose in unison and roared with approving applause.

As a member of the National Speakers Association, I've had the opportunity to meet, hear, and work with many of the world's most celebrated speakers. At the Association's 1990 Awards Banquet in the Atlanta Marriott's Marquis Ballroom, my wife and I sat with Dr. and Mrs. Peale at dinner. This isn't normally a celebrity-hungry group, but the members sure went crazy over Dr. Peale.

After dinner Dr. Peale was called to the stage so he could announce that his friend and one of our colleagues, Michael Frank, had been selected to receive the Council of Peers Award of Excellence, the highest award accorded for speaking skills and professionalism. As Dr. Peale's name was announced, all 1500 tuxedoed and bejeweled professional speakers present for the banquet rose and applauded.

After his presentation, another speaker and I carefully helped the venerable gentleman down off the platform. As the audience prolonged its applause, the nonagenarian turned to me and my partner and quietly said with a chuckle,

"You look like you're practicing to be pallbearers!" It was the only reference I heard him make to his age that whole evening, and he certainly meant it jokingly.

Later, I asked Dr. Peale for his prescription for enjoying life at such an advanced age. He said, simply, "Live your life and forget your age."

Many people hex their happiness by talking about how old they are. It seems that hitting their 40th birthday triggers a stream of "I'm getting old" exclamations that continues for the next 40 or so years. Why do many celebrities conceal or falsify their ages, as if acknowledgment of their years would lower their esteem in their fans' eyes? It's not a person's chronological age that matters, it's his attitude toward aging that makes all the difference.

Webster's Ninth New Collegiate Dictionary defines "youthful" as: "Having accomplished or undergone little erosion." Losing youthfulness is a process of erosion, and we do much of it to ourselves. We wear away our own self-images by commenting disparagingly about our advancing age. We send supposedly funny birthday cards that deride our friends as they mark the anniversaries of their birth. The collective effect of all these comments is to erode our feelings of youthfulness.

Just as there's no point in hastening your own erosion, why contribute to anyone else's feeling of "getting too old"? I recommend boycotting the greeting cards that make disparaging jokes about aging. Although meant in jest, they merely contribute to a collective consciousness that sees aging as a negative condition. Even if they're hard to find, scan your greeting card shelves and look for those cards that help buoy your friends and relatives as they get on in years.

QUICK REFERENCE

What you can do right now:
Use neutral or positive phrases in reference to advancing age. Don't erode vitality by speaking negatively about aging.

Instead of saying,

"I'm going downhill, my hair is graying, wrinkles are showing, and I look like an old bag."

Say,

"I keep myself in shape and I look good."

Instead of saying,

"At my age, you know, it's just too hard to have any fun anymore. My old body is giving out on me."

Say,

"At my age, I enjoy different kinds of fun. What did you have in mind?"

Instead of saying,

"I feel worse and worse. I'm getting too old."

Say,

"I feel good."

III. Rebound Resiliently

Power Talkers rebound resiliently. Sure, they experience set-backs, and they bounce right back from them. They learn from their experiences and emerge stronger than they were going in. Ever notice how many truly wealthy people have been flat broke or even bankrupt at one or more times as they accumulated their wealth? They didn't give up. They learned, and rebounded resiliently.

In Section II, I discussed Dr. Martin Seligman's research dealing with the "explanatory styles" and language characteristics of optimists and pessimists. There, we examined how Power Talkers describe *positive* events. When things go *badly*, the Power Talker uses the opposite explanatory style. He concentrates on specific, external, and temporary explanations. The power*less* talker sees problems as being universal ("Not only is this situation not working out, but everything in my life is awful"), internal ("It's all my fault, I'm a loser"), and permanent ("Things never go my way, and this is just another example that proves it").

As a Power Talker, when you experience negative situations in life—when you lose a job, or your promotion doesn't come through, or your child has a difficult time in school—you consciously replace universal, internal, and permanent explanations with those that are specific, external, and temporary. When a Power Talker doesn't get that big promotion, he says,

> "I missed out on that promotion, and I understand way. I haven't yet mastered the new inventory forecasting software, and it's really vital that I learn to use it well. I know I can, once I go through the training tutorial. I've had plenty of career successes in the past, and more great things are right around the corner for me. I'm certainly glad that I'm doing so well in the other areas of my life. My health is superb, my family relationships are great, and I have excellent job skills. I know that I'm ripe for career advancement, and will begin now working toward that next big jump."

It's entirely natural to respond negatively when things go wrong; I often do it myself. Don't expect the Power Talking principles to come naturally. Work at them.

In the chapters ahead, you're going to meet people who have rebounded from disastrous situations. They've changed bankruptcies, personal failures, alcoholism, depression, and smaller setbacks into positive experiences. You may be confronted with a variety of setbacks today, yourself. When they happen, use the Power Talking phrases in the following chapters and you'll come out ahead.

18. Does Your History Repeat Itself?

You get fired from your job. You're two payments behind on your mortgage. Your spouse walks out.

Say out loud to yourself:

"I know why this is happening to me: I'm a failure."

Now, say:

"I know there's an important lesson in all of this. What can I learn?"

Which sounds like the person who will go down for the count? Which is the winner who will learn valuable lessons from these circumstances and emerge wiser and stronger?

How would you feel if, at age 40, after 20 years of abundant business success, you had to call your father and ask him to loan you $400 . . . so you could afford to file for personal bankruptcy?

In the mid 1970s, Michael McCafferty left his position as a successful salesman at IBM in order to start his own business. He did very well with the Philadelphia-based computer service bureau he founded, and operated it profitably for seven years. It was acquired by a larger firm, and the President of the new parent company reached a handshake agreement with Michael that would make him a very rich man.

But first, the President died. It was then that Michael realized his agreement had never been put in writing. The new corporate officers decided not to honor it, and Michael was cheated out of his promised stock.

Humiliated, he packed up and left for Chicago, where he successfully ran another service bureau three times larger and "cashed out" after two years. Chicago's winters were just too much for him, so Michael, in his mid-30s, headed for San Diego, got a place at the beach, bought a vintage Ferrari, and lived a wonderful, carefree life. It got boring. That's when an old business associate approached him about starting a new venture.

Michael was intrigued. He coupled his mastery of computers with a recognition that people will always want convenient access to more information. He created the first Electronic Yellow Pages system and perfected the technology that is today still the basis for a growing industry.

Then his partner got cold feet and pulled out. Michael had no doubt that the business would be a big success and decided to invest further, on his own. He sold the Ferrari and bought a battered 1972 Vega. Then he gave up his place at the beach. And before long, every dime he had was invested in the failing business.

While Michael was reeking of desperation, a shark caught his scent. A fast-talking moneyman offered to rescue the company and get Michael back on his feet . . . for a 51% share of the company. Other partners were brought in and Michael's business crumbled.

Michael McCafferty quit working and sank into a deep depression. He had no income and lived off his credit cards. Bankruptcy was his only way out, but he couldn't afford the court filing charge! So his dad bailed him out one last time.

For a full year Michael repeatedly said to himself,

"Why me? What happened to my money, my Ferrari, my carefree early retirement? How come that fast-talking moneyman wound up with everything?"

His all-consuming thought was, "Why did this happen to me?" After a year of destitution, desperation, and depression, the answer dawned on him: "Because I let it." It was that simple. The world hadn't victimized him, he had invited his misfortune. He had trusted the wrong people, he'd behaved naively, he didn't get important agreements in writing, and he gave up authority.

He had conceded control. Not just financial ownership of the company, but control of his fate, too. He gave up control of everything by thinking that things were "happening to him."

Once he realized what the lesson was, he got to work. He read Og Mandino's classic, *The Greatest Salesman in the World*, and wrote out its affirmations on a 3 x 5 card:

> **"Today I begin a new life.**
> **I will persist until I succeed.**
> **I will live this day as if it is my last.**
> **I will act now."**

He read them aloud first thing in the morning, last thing before bed, and several times during the day.

Michael looked back on his "failures" and drew lessons from them. He distilled them into "The Ten Commandments for Managing a Young Growing Business," and he made a commitment to obey them. On St. Patrick's Day, 1983, he founded a new company and named it Remote Control (of course). As I write this book, Michael's company has grown at an average annual rate of 133% over the last seven years. Based on the lessons he learned from his multiple "failures," he created the top selling software package in its category, "TeleMagic." It helps hundreds of thousands of sales professionals around the world become more organized, more profitable, and maintain control. Finally, Michael McCafferty is the multimillionaire he deserves to be. From his perch at the edge of the ocean in Del Mar, California, he watches the dolphins and pelicans and is grateful that he learned his lessons.

Power Talkers consciously recognize that failing is a vital part of succeeding. When they say "I failed!" it has an exclamation mark after it, and is closely followed by, "And here's what I learned." Losers just say, "I failed." It's followed by a period. As Vince Lombardi said,

"It's not whether you get knocked down. It's whether you get up again."

Michael McCafferty got up again and drew invaluable lessons from his mistakes.

Don't fear failures, welcome them. May you have many, and learn important lessons from them all.

QUICK REFERENCE

What you can do right now:
When you're confronted with a "failure," look for the lessons you can learn and grow from the experience.

Instead of saying,

"What a stupid move. How could I have scraped together my entire life savings and spent it to build a spec house, only to discover that the market was already turning sour? I'm a complete failure."

Say,

"Putting all my eggs in one basket didn't pay off, and this investment has not produced an acceptable profit. I've learned some valuable lessons, though, and I'm not going to take an uninformed risk like that again."

Instead of saying,

"That's the fourth job interview I've had and again they didn't even call me back or send a letter. I must be a failure."

Say,

"My approach to these job interviews hasn't been working. One thing I've learned is that the interviewers

don't call me back. Maybe that means I should take the initiative and follow up with them. After the next one, I'm going to immediately send a thank you note."

Instead of saying,

"I failed."

Say,

"Here's what I learned . . ."

19. Half Empty, or Half Full?

You've been working closely with an influential Director in your organization for the last five years. Your current major project is critically important to your future, and the Director has been your "coach" and prime backer. She calls you into her office and announces that she's accepted another position with a leading organization in your field.

Say out loud to yourself:

"Now what'll I do? She believes in me and fully supports me on this project, but she's leaving. Now I'm high and dry. I'll have to start over with someone new. This is a major setback for me."

Now, say:

"Now that she's leaving, I'll continue our association and keep her as a good contact outside our company.

And I'll be able to develop a strong new relationship with her replacement. This is an interesting change."

Which sounds like the person who's going to feel depressed and go into a career "holding pattern"? Who's going to eagerly dive in and capitalize on a new set of circumstances?

In the publishing world, an author's most important contact is the editor. This is the person who believes in the writer and supports the book project right from the start. The editor negotiates the author's book advance and many other critical elements of the contract. Once the publisher has committed to producing the book, the author relies on the editor as the internal spokesperson; the editor orchestrates publicity, promotion, and sales support.

The editor who championed my first book, *Phone Power*, also initiated this one. With the *Power Talking* manuscript half finished, she called to tell me she had accepted a position with another publisher.

My immediate reaction was:

"That may be a great career move for her, but what a setback for me! Now I'll have to start all over at the bottom and work with an editor I've never even met. Maybe that person won't even like my book. What if she abandons it and lets the sales force ignore it?"

You know the old saying about the glass: It's either half-empty or half-full, depending entirely on how you look at it. I was looking at my glass and seeing risks, downside potential, and nothing but problems.

I hope you don't think that Power Talking comes easily or automatically for me or for anyone else. It requires concerted, constant attention and effort. Five minutes after hearing this "bad news," I got up from my computer keyboard, walked to the window of my writing office and, looking out at the stream and woods, forced myself to say,

"What great news! Now I'll have a strong advocate at another publishing house. When I meet my new editor, I'll get to 'sell' her on *Power Talking* so she's full of enthusiasm right from the start. Instead of presenting a half-formed idea, I can show her exactly what the book's about. And, with her fresh perspective, she'll probably offer plenty of new promotional ideas."

As I look back now, I can see that my editor's departure opened many new opportunities for me. The glass was half-full—and filling.

When confronted with any situation that represents a change in what we're accustomed to and planning on, most of us naturally see the negative side first. I do it often myself. The trick is to recognize that seeing the negative "half-empty" aspect first doesn't mean that's the only way you can, or will, look at it.

Seeing that the glass is half-full is a learned skill. Don't feel discouraged if it doesn't come immediately or naturally. Do use the power of your language to turn things around.

Be on the lookout. Whenever "this is bad news because . . ." crops up in your comments to yourself or others, stop and replace that line of thinking with, "This is good news because . . ." You can't exploit opportunities if you don't see them. Train yourself to see the good side by using a fill-in-the-blanks technique. Force yourself to complete the sentence: "There's a good side to this situation, and it's what I choose to focus on. This is great news because . . ."

QUICK REFERENCE

What you can do right now:
Rephrase negative reactions to unexpected changes and say, "This is great news. It means that . . . ," and then start looking for the positive result that can follow.

Instead of saying,

"I didn't get the promotion; that's terrible news."

Say,

"I didn't get the promotion, and that's good news because it means I can expand my horizons. I'm going to make a few calls and see what my talents are worth to some other companies. Then I'll have a better idea of how well off I am right here."

Instead of saying,

"Darn, our house sale fell through. Now we have to start all over again."

Say,

"OK, that buyer backed out. I'm glad it happened now instead of at the last minute. This means we can reappraise the market conditions and be sure our pricing strategy makes the most of this present situation."

Instead of saying,

"The car repairs won't be completed by noon, as the dealer promised. That screws up my whole schedule."

Say,

"Since the car won't be ready by noon, I'm going to take this opportunity to walk over to the branch library down the street from the dealership. I haven't been there for ages. It's a good thing that my plans have changed."

Instead of saying,

"I see some very negative consequences resulting from this turn of events."

Say,

"I see some very positive consequences resulting from this turn of events."

20. If Only I Had . . .

You attend your trade association's annual convention and, upon reading the program carefully, realize that tomorrow night's Awards Banquet is a black-tie event. Your tux is hanging in the closet at home.

Say out loud to yourself:

"If only I had read the program more carefully before I packed. Why don't I ever plan ahead for these things? I'm going to look completely out of place."

Now, say:

"I'll check with the concierge and see about a last-minute tuxedo rental. Next time I'll be sure to carefully read the program materials several days before attending my convention."

Which sounds like the person who's bound to have a miserable time at the Awards Banquet and may well repeat the experience next year?

A coronary bypass operation can really make you stop and think. For a friend of mine, it also prompted a host of "If only I had . . ." regrets. In his early 40s, this young man had concentrated on his career, dedicated far too little attention to his family, and ignored common nutritional guidelines.

From his hospital bed, Jerry kept talking about his regrets: "If only I had spent more time with my kids." "If only I had avoided all those high-cholesterol foods." "If only I had led a more balanced life."

To hear him talk, you'd have thought he was writing his own epitaph. Despite the successful surgery, Jerry was still heading down the wrong path. He was dwelling on his regrets and wishing for what might have been, rather than concentrating on mending his ways and aiming for an improved quality of life.

Jerry's turnaround began when his "If only I had . . ." statements ended. He agreed to delete the powerless phrase from his vocabulary, and his family and friends helped reinforce the point by interrupting whenever he started to say, "If only I had . . ." Soon Jerry was saying, "I haven't enjoyed my family as much as I deserve, and I'm changing that, starting now." "I haven't been sensible about my eating habits, and I'm now beginning a healthy, nutritious diet." "I've been out of balance, and now I'm consciously working toward a balanced life."

Today Jerry is like a new man. It wasn't just the arterial operation that did it. His verbal surgery played an important role, too. You don't need a doctor's help to begin surgically removing your own "If only I had . . ." regrets.

When you hear someone using the phrase "If only I had . . . ," you can usually be sure that his gaze is fixed on the past. He's floundering in regrets, preoccupied with what can't be changed. The appropriate time to talk about a regrettable past is when you're conducting a retrospective analysis of what went wrong so you can fix it.

In my travels I've occasionally had my checked luggage lost or delayed and once even went onstage wearing tennis shoes and jeans. When that happened, I wished I had taken my luggage on board with me. I've also hand-carried my bulging garment bag, lugged it from gate B-1 to gate E-32 while running for a close connection, and wished that I had carried on nothing but my briefcase. In each case it would have been easy to get bogged down in "If only I had . . ." thinking.

Rather than dwelling on the past and regretting my actions, I've used these experiences to focus on the future: "When I pack and check all of my business clothing, I risk losing it; when I carry it on, I'm bogged down. So starting now I will find a better answer." My solution has been to check all of my luggage, including the fresh suit I plan to wear onstage. I fly wearing another suit that I could use for my presentation if my bags are lost. For footwear I choose comfortable black Reebok sneakers and carry a black marking pen. In a pinch I can ink over the white logo and my shoes will "pass."

If a salesperson just barely misses winning the regional sales contest, you can easily assess her likelihood of triumphing in the future based on how she describes her loss. If she says, "If only I had sold 5% more, I could be in Acapulco next January. What a bad break," her prospects are poor. If she says, "I was just 5% short of winning, and I'm sure I can be 5% more effective by qualifying my sales prospects more carefully. Next time I'll be more productive," you're hearing a winner.

The same "If only I had . . ." phrasing is common to managers, negotiators, and other professionals who consistently fall short of their potential. In fact, most anyone who says "If only I had . . ." is probably holding himself back from more fully succeeding in any endeavor from selling to parenting.

Help yourself eliminate negative, regret-filled retrospecting by doing away with the phrase "If only I had . . ." Replace it with a positive, forward-looking statement like "Starting now, I will . . ."

QUICK REFERENCE

What you can do right now:
Focus your attention—and your language—on what you will do to positively shape your future. Don't dwell on the unalterable past by talking about what might have been.

Instead of saying,

"If only I had held on to my Mustang for a few more years, I could have sold it for a lot of money as a classic."

Say,

"Next time I buy a car with appreciation potential I'll check the outlook before I sell it."

Instead of saying,

"Maybe we could have had a family if only I had been more family-oriented before my wife's hysterectomy. Now it's too late."

Say,

"I'd still like to have a family. We can look into adoption agencies or find out about becoming foster parents."

Instead of saying,

"If only I had."

Say,

"Starting now, I will."

21. Bottoming Out

Your life has slipped downhill. First you were demoted, then you started drinking, then your marriage crumbled.

Say out loud to yourself:

"I shouldn't have to go through this mess. I know things should be better for me, I just don't know where or how to start."

Now, say:

"I will change my life. I will start making things better today, right now. Nobody else will do it. I will take action."

Which sounds like the person who will wait and wait for something to happen, and later wonder why it never did? Who will start taking action and begin moving in the right direction?

For "Tom," it all boils down to a single truth:

"You can act yourself into right thinking, but you can't think yourself into right action."

When you hit bottom, you can't think your way out of it. You must **do something.** And for Tom, the most effective action was to change his language.

I met Tom while I lived at Venice Beach, California. Most who've heard of it think of Venice as an artsy, chic community. Movie producers, famous artists, and Beverly Hills rebels move there to be offbeat.

There's another side to Venice. Hippies who never quite moved out of the 60s live in ramshackle bungalows and drive phychedelically painted Beetles. The coexist with a violent community of hard drug users. It was there that Tom hit bottom. He was unemployed, broke, living in a slum neighborhood, stumbling along to the next bottle of wine, the next pill. He didn't realize he was an alcoholic until he totally burned out physically and emotionally.

Tom's life began to turn around when he met an Alcoholics Anonymous member who dragged him to his first meeting. By all outward appearances, Tom was indisputably a loser when he began the 12 steps of recovery procedure that's common to AA programs around the world.

His new sober friends helped him with support and faith. They encouraged him to adopt an attitude of Positive Expectancy. They told him to visualize what he wanted his life to be like, and he did. He concentrated on seeing himself as a successful, sober person. He wasn't sure *how* he would become successful; he just had faith that the way would become clear if he concentrated on the end rather than the means.

Then Tom's liver failed. Admitted to St. John's Hospital in Santa Monica, he lay in bed and reflected. He knew he wanted to be successful, he held an attitude of Positive Expectancy, he was thinking himself toward his goal, but he wasn't seeing any action. Looking back now, Tom views his hospital stay as a blessing. He had the time—sober—to really figure out his feelings. He concluded that there was a saboteur at work inside him. He'd visualize a goal, and then his lifetime of angry feelings took over and prevented him from reaching it.

It hit Tom with a flash: "Affirmations are worthless without action."

So, he began to **do**, not just think. He began writing out his affirmations:

"I, Tom, dare to be prosperous."
"I, Tom, relentlessly visualize success in every endeavor—and I act to make it so."

"I, Tom, reject, nullify, void, and veto all thoughts of
failure."
"Failure will never overtake me if my desire to succeed
is strong enough, and I act on that desire."

Then, there in the hospital, he began repeating them to
himself, over and over again. Soon after his release, Tom
landed a new job. A new friend who was a great salesman
encouraged him to pursue a career in the sales profession, so
Tom went to work for a small company that sold computer
printer ribbons by phone. He applied himself, took action,
and—one day at a time—became the top salesman.

Tom eventually left to start his own company.

Still repeating his affirmations, he lay on Venice Beach
and visualized a room with 40 people, all producing profitable sales, all working for him. He started small, rolling out of
bed, eating a bowl of cereal, and making the sales calls himself from his small apartment.

Today Tom is president of a company that sells computer
ribbons to half of the Fortune 500 companies, manufactures
a line of top-quality computer products in its 30,000-square-
foot production facility, and employs 130 people. Annual
sales exceed $15 million. Tom has a talented, loving, sup-
portive wife (whom he met through the AA program), a
young son, and a balanced life. When work pressures mount,
he rewards himself by taking his family to a remote area of
Idaho, where they own a rustic log cabin originally hand-
built by a famous movie star. As Tom says, "It's not where
you start, it's where you finish."

Tom's story isn't unique. Tens of thousands live lives as
rich as his, and have rebounded from circumstances as dis-
mal as his, too. They all have one thing in common: They
didn't just decide to turn their lives around—they took action.

If you are at a low point in your life, take action. Begin by
saying—not just thinking—what you want to be true. Use

the power of affirmations and spoken words to move yourself toward the success you deserve. Lao-Tzu didn't remind us to think about taking steps, he wrote, simply:

"A journey of a thousand miles begins with one step."

QUICK REFERENCE

What you can do right now:
When you're at a low point, write out your affirmations, using positive language, and say them aloud to yourself. Don't just think, act.

Instead of saying,

"I'm failure-prone. Look at what a mess I've made of my life already."

Say,

"Failure will never overtake me if my desire to succeed is strong enough, and I act upon it."

Instead of saying,

"I'm visualizing myself as a successful person, putting my troubles behind me. But nothing is changing."

Say,

"Today, I am taking action. I am moving toward the success I deserve to make of myself."

Instead of thinking to yourself,

"I'm a loser."

Say,

"I am a winner."

22. Bouncing Back

You're managing a department that's threatened with extensive layoffs. Just when your workers need strong emotional support and effective representation, they discover that the union official representing their local has skipped off to Barbados with a big chunk of the retirement fund. A "workers' committee" asks to meet with you to discuss what the future holds.

Say out loud to yourself:

"I don't know what to tell you people. It looks bad, and I just don't see how things are going to turn around."

Now, say:

"I understand how uncertain you must be feeling, and I know we're facing big challenges. We've overcome hurdles before, and we'll make it out of this present situation, too. We are a strong team, and we will bounce back. I know we'll be able to come up with a good plan for turning things around by working together."

Which sounds like the manager whose team will get busy and start thinking of solutions? Which is about to face a worsening situation with morale declining and productivity sinking?

At 3:00 on a Friday afternoon, the movers arrived with empty cardboard boxes. The locksmith walked toward the VP's office with a drill and began changing the lock. Word spread quickly.

Barbara Grego was the Telemarketing Manager for House of Almonds, then a wholly owned subsidiary of Tenneco. She led her department to grow from four people to 27 in one single season. The company had discovered that salespeople could phone corporate gift buyers and secure very profitable orders for Almond Gift Packs. They weren't selling nuts so much as convenience. Companies that traditionally sent gifts to their customers during the holiday season could bypass shopping, gift wrapping, and shipping by turning to House of Almonds. They'd mail or fax their customer address lists, indicate which ones should get which category of present, jot out what the gift cards should say, and House of Almonds took it from there.

The prime selling season spanned just a few months, from August through November. The pressure was intense during this time; tension and stress plagued the department. Facing some critical challenges over internal funding, and undergoing the normal growing pains any department would experience during a 500% expansion, Barbara called me in as a consultant to advise her on management issues and train her rapidly growing telemarketing team. One of the telemarketing department's prime assets within the organization was a vice president who believed in Barbara's management. Then, at the peak of the crunch, he was given his walking papers.

As her mentor's office was cleared out, Barbara's reaction was to plaster the word "Buoyant" throughout the department. She thumbtacked banners to the wall and had key chains made for every employee. They all said just one word: "Buoyant."

Barbara Grego wanted to remind her staff—and herself—that they were buoyant. Life has its ups and downs, and if there were no challenges or upsets, it would be mighty dull.

Power Talkers recognize that during the tough times they grow stronger. Sure, circumstances seem to conspire and push us briefly underwater from time to time. When they do, it's easy to feel as if we're drowning. The key is to remember that adversity tests our mettle, giving us an opportunity to surface again, stronger and wiser.

The bleakest circumstances often precede a promising change of events. It's crucial to picture yourself, and the team you lead—whether that's your family or a work group—rising above the storm, getting your head back above water. Picturing it isn't enough. Talk about it. Let the words you use reflect your determination to hang in there with the expectation that things will improve.

QUICK REFERENCE

What you can do right now:
When you hear yourself describing a setback situation as a terminal disaster, rephrase your description to recognize that you will bounce back and move ahead.

Instead of saying,

"My department's been slashed, my mentor has been fired, and my career's going into a nosedive."

Say,

"I'm buoyant enough to surface from this turbulent situation. Experiences like these are what strengthen my talents as a manager."

Instead of saying,

"Since my best friend moved to the West Coast, I feel at a loss. I just don't see how I'll ever get past this loneliness."

Say,

"I really miss Nicole since she moved. Now I'm going to call Judy and start getting to know her. I know I'll make new friends."

Instead of saying,

"I've damaged the tendons in my foot and the doctor says I'll never play racquetball again."

Say,

"I'm going to really take care of myself so my foot will heal quickly. Then I'll find a sport that won't be so hard on my feet."

Instead of saying,

"I'm going under."

Say,

"I'm going to bounce back."

23. It's Over!

You've just returned home from a two-week vacation. Unlocking the front door, you find that your home's burglar alarm has been activated. You're sure you set it before leaving and fear that someone may have broken in sometime while you were away.

Say out loud to yourself:

"Oh no! What if we've been burglarized? They've probably stolen my jewelry! And what if they've taken the computer with all my records on the hard disk? If they've got my Daytimer, I'm in a real jam. What am I going to do?"

Now, say:

"We may have been burglarized, so let's carefully check all through the house. If valuables are missing, insurance will replace most of them. Let's do a thorough inventory."

Who's the best candidate for an ulcer? Which person do you want to be around when a real emergency occurs?

Stew Leonard approached the woman at the airport's Hertz counter and asked, "Have you seen a giant yellow chicken wandering around here?" The rental agent laughed and said, "No, as a matter of fact, I haven't." So Stew asked, "Which way to the escalator?" The rental agent replied, "Escalator? There's no escalator at this airport."

Stew Leonard founded and built the world's largest dairy store, according to Ripley's Believe It or Not. Tom Peters made him famous around the world when he extolled Stew's brand of customer service in his "Excellence" books and video. Tom Peters said, "I've searched the world over looking for excellence in every nook and cranny. One of the best examples I found was a dairy store in Norwalk, Connecticut . . . Stew Leonard's."

Stew was en route to be the keynote speaker at a conference on quality presented by Frank Perdue of Perdue Chicken. Frank holds an annual conference with notable guest speakers and invites his most important customers, suppliers, and key staff members to attend. This particular conference was being held at Amelia Island, an exclusive resort off the coast of Florida near Jacksonville.

In confirming the arrangements, Frank had said, "Stew, don't worry about a thing. As soon as you step off the plane, I'll have someone in a giant yellow chicken costume waiting by the escalator to meet you. The chicken will escort you right to the limousine. The island resort is connected to the mainland by a bridge and it's only an hour's drive from the Jacksonville airport."

But when Stew stepped off his plane, there was no chicken waiting to greet him. So he proceeded to the baggage claim area. After watching all the other passengers claim their bags and leave, the carousel came to a stop, and Stew thought, "No chicken, and now no luggage! My clothes, my slides, my notes, everything I need is in my suitcase."

He finally decided to rent a car on his own, head out to the island, and make arrangements for lost luggage later. When he asked the Hertz agent how long the drive would take, she advised him it would take several hours. "Several hours?" But Frank Perdue told me that the island is less than an hour away from Jacksonville!" She replied, "That's true, but we're not in Jacksonville, Florida. This is Savannah, Georgia!"

Stew suddenly realized that he had gotten off his one-stop flight to Jacksonville prematurely, at the intermediate stop. His luggage had gone on along with the plane to Jacksonville without him.

Stew paused for a minute and considered the situation. Within the hour his plane would be landing in Jacksonville without him; the passengers would stream off and notice a man in a chicken costume in the arrival area. The limousine driver would be faithfully waiting at the bottom of the escalator as Stew's unclaimed luggage circled on the carousel.

Stew followed his own prescription for dealing with setback situations: He laughed for a moment and said to himself, "It's over!" There was no point in dwelling on the situation or circumstances; it would help nothing at all to beat himself up for having gotten off the plane too soon. Instead he used his time and energy to contact Frank Perdue to be sure someone picked up his luggage in Jacksonville. He then made his way directly to the island via chartered airplane.

As Stew told me the story, he said: "My policy is that whenever there's absolutely nothing to be gained by dwelling on the stupidity of a situation, whenever something really bad happens and it seems like all my plans are ruined, I just say to myself, 'It's over.' That's my secret for making the best of the situation. In this way I save my energy to make things better. As it turned out, the plane I chartered got me to the island in plenty of time. My bags were delivered to the hotel, I had a great new story to add to my talk, and the program was a success."

Stew Leonard's advice reminds me of the most helpful book I read in high school. It was Dale Carnegie's classic, *How to Stop Worrying and Start Living*. In it he suggests a simple three-step process for ending fears and worries. It goes like this:

1. Identify exactly what it is that you're worried about and answer this question: What is the very worst thing that could happen as a result of this situation?

2. Accept "the worst" as if it were a reality. Visualize that it has already occurred. Having now accepted your worst fears, there is no need to expend any of your energy worrying about having them come true. They have come true!

3. Redirect the energy that you had been using to worry about your worst fears coming true, and now, instead, do something useful that will help prevent them from materializing.

I've used that simple formula in a wide range of situations and have found that it never fails. Let's put it to work in Stew's predicament.

1. *What's the very worst that could happen?* Well, Stew could have found that there were no charter flights available and realized that it was impossible for him to reach the island in time for his program. He could have missed it altogether and disappointed his friend Frank Perdue. The audience would also have been disappointed. Stew would not have been able to accept his professional speaking fee for the engagement and might well have suffered some financial penalty. He would have returned home to Connecticut knowing that he had disappointed his friend and his audience. If that had happened, Frank would probably have seen the humorous side of the situation, entertained the audi-

ence himself, and the conference would have gone ahead with an altered agenda.

2. *Accept "the worst" as if it were true.* In his mind's eye, Stew would visualize Frank Perdue walking onstage the following morning and announcing to the audience that Stew had gotten off the flight one stop too soon and wouldn't be able to give his talk. They would have muttered in disappointment and probably also laughed about the circumstances. Although unlikely, Stew might also have gotten a phone call from Frank chewing him out for missing the engagement.

Would Stew be in physical pain? No. Would his career be threatened? No. Would his personal fortunes be ruined? Of course not. He would have disappointed his friend and the audience and suffered a financial loss. That's all. Accepting this, Stew would still want to carry on—and leave this mistake in the past.

3. *Now use the energy that you might have fretted away and do something constructive.* This is exactly what Stew did. He got on the phone, made the charter flight arrangements, notified Frank, and everything turned out just fine.

In this situation the complexities of the backup arrangements were such that a few minutes' delay could have made all the difference. The charter aircraft might not have been available a short while later. The pilot could have gone home for the day. The small, unlit airport at Stew's island destination might have shut down for the night. Had Stew paced around the airport bemoaning his situation and berating himself for making a stupid mistake, the "worst that could happen" might well have actually happened.

Think of how many times you've seen people drain their energy by constantly rehashing the details of a negative situation they're in. This cannot make things any better, and may well make them a lot worse. At the very least, the worrying and moaning makes everyone involved feel lousy. When you're in a predicament, accept circumstances as they are and use your energy to move ahead in a positive direction.

QUICK REFERENCE

What you can do right now:
When things seem to be headed for a disastrous outcome, stop and ask yourself, "What's the very worst thing that could happen?" Accept that eventuality as if it were true and say, "That's all; it's over." Then, get to work applying your energy to create a more positive outcome.

Instead of saying,

"It looks like I won't be able to finish the report on time, and I just dread having to face my boss if it's not done. I can just imagine what he's going to do if I don't finish on time."

Say,

"I may not be able to complete the report on time. The worst that could happen is the boss will be disappointed and ask me to stay here late until it's finished. He's not going to fire me, he'll just be upset. That's all; it's over. Now, I'll work on outlining the remaining sections of the report so I have a good structure to show him."

Instead of saying,

"What rotten luck! I cut my hand just before the volleyball championships. Now I can't play and my team will probably lose. It'll be all my fault."

Say,

"With this cut on my hand, playing volleyball is out of the question. I'm the best spiker on the team and with-

out me, we may lose. That's all. Since I can't play, I'm going to coach Ron so he'll improve his spiking."

Instead of saying,

"This is terrible, and it could get a lot worse."

Say,

"Even if the worst happened, I could live with it. So there's no point worrying. That's all; it's over. Now I'm going to work on making things better."

IV. Accept Responsibility

Power Talkers eagerly accept personal responsibility. They put themselves on the line. Rather than blaming others and holding them accountable, Power Talkers see themselves as being in control of their fate. They're not victims and they don't talk as if they're casualties of circumstances beyond their control.

Power Talkers shape their circumstances. When they're not optimal, they get busy and change them. When a situation is truly not changeable, the Power Talker actively manages his own reaction to the circumstances.

In these coming chapters, you'll meet people who guide their own fates, who are masters of their own ships. They apply Power Talking language to very significant situations, like a crippling motorcycle accident, and to seemingly insignificant situations, like being "too busy" to relax with a good book. You're about to see how Power Talkers show others—and themselves—that they are responsible.

24. Watch Where You Point That Thing!

You're breaking in a new employee who shows excellent potential. He still seems confused about a few of the office procedures you've explained several times during training.

Say out loud to yourself:

"You make me so frustrated! I've explained this job over and over and you just can't seem to get it right."

Now, say:

"I feel frustrated when we don't understand each other. What areas shall I explain a little more clearly?"

Which statement is more likely to encourage cooperation? Which will result in changes that improve the situation?

My mother, Edith, used a lot of homespun adages that still make sense. In my mind's eye, I can see her smiling and pointing. As a kid, when I made an excuse for not completing my homework assignments on time, she'd extend the index finger of her right hand, curl back the other three fingers, and point at my imaginary excuse. If I said I couldn't complete a book report because my typewriter was jammed, she'd break into her radiant smile and, with a twinkle in her eye, emphatically point at the poor old Smith-Corona and wiggle her other three fingers. This was her way of reminding me that my attention should be concentrated on those other three fingers because they were pointing back at *me*. My index finger identified only the object of *imagined* responsibility.

Her pointing motion cued me to rephrase my description of the predicament. Instead of saying,

"The typewriter is jammed, and I can't use it, so I can't complete my report on time,"

I'd look at the other three fingers and remember to redirect my attention back to myself, and my role, by saying:

"I didn't plan ahead and check the typewriter. Since it's jammed, I'll be hand-writing my book report tonight and will get the typewriter fixed tomorrow."

Salespeople tend to gripe about customers who don't buy:

"That cheapskate can't see past the purchase price. He can't even understand that in the long run our equipment is less expensive to own and operate and will serve him better."

Where's that salesman's index finger pointing? At the customer. When he redirects his attention to the other three fingers, the scene changes:

"I still haven't convinced my prospect that the long-term operating costs are a more important consideration than the up-front price. I'll use another approach and make it more clear."

If he stays focused on his index finger, there's not much else he can do but look for another prospect. He discards the first nonbuyer after declaring him defective. What he's really saying is:

"If that prospect can't see beyond the purchase price, it's his own fault. He's not smart enough and doesn't deserve to become my customer anyway!"

Paying attention to the other three fingers is much more productive. We can't really change our prospects or customers. We can alter our own behavior. If we set out to change others, we're likely to become more and more frustrated and disgusted about short-sighted prospects. When we concentrate on changing ourselves, we improve our own sales techniques and become more and more effective.

The old finger-pointing routine is especially relevant to emotional proclamations:

"You're driving me crazy!"

Really? The other person is forcing you, against your will, to lose control and go insane?

I've taught many seminars for Customer Service professionals who deal with a steady stream of emotional callers. It's tempting for them to say,

"Those rude callers make me so mad! They raise their voices, they swear, and they imply that I've loused up their accounts, even though I had nothing to do with it. They make me furious."

The reality is, some callers do raise their voices, curse, and make inaccurate accusations. But they don't make anybody mad. Mad people make themselves mad by reacting to stimuli. It's not the other person's fault.

Redirecting attention to where the other three fingers are pointing—to yourself—changes the situation:

"When callers raise their voices and say certain words, I become upset. I need to depersonalize those situations. Some specific words and behaviors trigger those reactions in me. I'm going to work on managing my reactions when I face those conditions in the future."

When you meet someone who's superb at handling upset people, notice how they concentrate on their own reactions to stimuli. They're paying attention to the other three fingers. Emotional confrontations result not so much from what other people do as from how we react to them.

Whether your goal is to manage your own emotions or communicate an important idea to a student, employee, or customer, focus on the three fingers that are pointing back to yourself. Changing the person or situation your index finger is pointing at is much more difficult and frustrating. You can always modify your own behavior.

QUICK REFERENCE

What you can do right now:
Be on the alert for that pointing finger! Whenever you hear (or see) yourself directing blame or responsibility elsewhere, focus on the three fingers that point back at you.

Instead of saying,

"He just doesn't seem to understand."

Say,

"I haven't yet made it clear."

Instead of saying,

"These customers just can't get it through their head that our price increase is reasonable and justified."

Say,

"I need to do a better job of explaining the justification for our price increase."

Instead of saying,

"You make me upset when . . ."

Say,

"I feel upset when . . ."

25. Use the Time You Have

The boss asks if you saw the article about your leading competitor in an industry trade journal. You've been working at full steam on an important analysis project and have fallen way behind on your reading.

Say out loud to yourself:

"No, I didn't see it. In fact, I never have enough time to do any of my industry reading when I'm working on a big project. I just can't seem to get through all my work and I'm constantly getting more and more behind. I don't know what I'm going to do."

Now, say:

"No, I haven't scheduled time to read the industry journals since I've been concentrating on the analysis project. I'd like to talk with you about our priorities and make sure that I'm scheduling my time in sync with your expectations."

Which sounds like someone who's in control of his time? Who is flailing about, using time inefficiently?

It doesn't take a time management expert to verify that you have available 1440 minutes every day and 525,600 minutes each year. How you use that time is purely a matter of choice. Some people are phenomenally productive and continually accomplish the many ambitious goals they set for themselves. Others achieve very little and when asked why, say, "There just isn't enough time."

When you say, "There isn't enough time," or, "I just haven't had the time," what you're really saying is that it's out of your control. You could accomplish more if you were given a few extra hours each day, but you haven't been granted that extra ration, so you can't get everything done. It's not your fault, you're a victim of time shortage!

Power Talkers accept responsibility for what they do accomplish, and for what they don't. Your achievements are a reflection of your choices about how you use time. Don't blame a failure to reach your goals on a lack of time.

I once shared the speaking platform with a medical doctor whose specialty is treating overstressed business executives. We were both addressing a conference of Sales and Marketing Executives in Buffalo, New York. The people in that audience were definitely stressed. They create ad campaigns, answer to their officers' (often unrealistic) sales goals, and implement and administer quotas.

In his 45-minute presentation, the doctor revealed that there's only one effective way to handle stress. Actually, he used 44 minutes to tell entertaining stories and one minute to prescribe his stress cure-all:

> **"I'm often called on to present a full-day seminar on stress management. Sometimes, though, the group has a tight schedule, so I can also cover it in a half-day version. If a client's budget is limited, I can do a two-hour program. Even a one-hour keynote speech is no problem. I've been studying and treating stress for many years and I have no doubt that I've found the answer. Since we have just a few minutes before my program ends, would you like to hear the ultracondensed version? In fact, would you like to know the one-sentence, surefire, cure-all technique that never fails to cure stress-related syndromes?** *If you want to have less stress in your life, lower your expectations.* **That's it. That's all there is to it."**

As blasphemous as this prescription sounded to his audience of high achievers, he confirmed that it was the only prescription that really works. Destructive stress results from setting unrealistic expectations. If we would all align what we want to accomplish with what we're realistically able to do, we'd have much less destructive stress.

Don't wish for more time. Take responsibility for how you use your available time and recognize that what you do and don't accomplish is a reflection of your choices. Remind yourself of that choice by talking about your time in terms that acknowledge your role in managing it.

QUICK REFERENCE

What you can do right now:
Purge phrases that suggest time is out of your control—that there's not enough of it. Acknowledge your personal responsibility with your language.

Instead of saying,

"I just haven't had enough time to finish it. I'm trying to get to it, but I just haven't ben able to. I need more time."

Say,

"I haven't yet finished it. I'm following my priorities, and that particular task is something I've scheduled for next week."

Instead of saying,

"This job is driving me crazy! They expect me to get twice as much done as I can possibly hope to accomplish. I can't say no when they give me a new assignment or they'll think I'm not really dedicated. Meanwhile I'm really burning out."

Say,

"I work better when I'm not feeling so stressed. My manager may not even realize how hard I'm working. I'm going to list the projects I'm working on and ask

him for some help in setting priorities. I'll explain what I can realistically accomplish and suggest that the lower-priority items be reassigned."

Instead of saying,

"I just can't get caught up; I don't have enough time."

Say,

"I can get caught up by managing my time and eliminating low-priority projects."

26. It's Not What Happens to You, It's What You Do About It

You're working on an important project that's right up on a deadline. One key element isn't ready, and the project may not be finished on time.

Say out loud to yourself:

"It's not my fault."

Now, say:

"It's my responsibility."

Which statement sounds like it's coming from someone who will take charge of his situation and make the best of it? Which comes from someone who's going to sit around blaming others for the situation he's in and do little to change it?

I'd never shaken a fingerless hand until I met W Mitchell. I first saw this unusual person at a National Speakers Association convention in San Antonio. I felt uncomfortable as soon as I noticed him across the hotel lobby. Confined to a wheelchair and grossly disfigured with extensive burns and scars, he was the kind of person who, because of his appearance, many of us choose to avoid.

When I saw him again, months later, at another convention, I still didn't summon the courage to approach "Mitchell," as he likes to be called. I consider myself a friendly, outgoing person, but just kept thinking how awkward I'd feel reaching out for his scarred hand. Thankfully, he wheeled over and shook mine. I now know one of the most beautiful people on this planet.

In the early seventies, Mitchell's motorcycle collided with a laundry truck in the middle of a busy San Francisco intersection. Passersby gasped as the cycle's gas tank burst open and Mitchell became a human fireball. Today, the only parts of his face that aren't scarred are thin strips of skin his helmet strap had protected.

After reconstructive surgery that included numerous grafts onto the stumps of his burned-off fingers and extensive physical therapy (not to mention months of excruciating pain), Mitchell bounced back. He qualified for his multiengine pilot's license; cofounded Vermont Castings, Inc., a highly successful metal-casting company employing over 400 people; ran for Congress; met with U.S. Presidents and Cabinet members; served as Mayor of a Colorado town; and enjoyed an active social life.

Then, while taking some friends up for a sightseeing flight, the small plane he was piloting crashed. As a result, Mitchell's burned, scarred, disfigured body was now also paralyzed from the waist down.

You'd think he would have just given up after this second

disaster. Instead he's gone on to become an extremely successful professional speaker. Mitchell wheels himself onto the stages of America's biggest sales meetings and conventions. He has appeared on the "Today" show, "Good Morning America," and "NBC Nightly News," and has been featured in *Time*, *Newsweek*, *Omni*, *Parade*, and *The New York Times*.

Mitchell is cheerful and productive, travels the world, manages extensive real estate investments, is happily married, and has a positive impact on a great many lives. How can he lead such a healthy life when he has so many handicaps, or "problems"?

"I have no problems," Mitchell says. "That's a foolish word. I do have many instances where unusual, challenging circumstances confront me. I am fully responsible for my present situation. Sure, the laundry truck driver was legally liable for the accident—and I'm responsible. I don't mean I'm guilty, or at fault. I am responsible—able to respond."

Mitchell sheds a whole new light on the concept of "blame." Many of us fall far short of achieving our potentials in life, and we often blame others. Can you think of friends who blame their parents, the educational system, a crooked business partner, or a multitude of other reasons for their situation? Do you do the same?

Power Talkers acknowledge that they are responsible. When we blame others, we weaken ourselves. Instead of improving our situation, we step backward. Other people and circumstances aren't what hold most of us back. *We* hold *ourselves* back because of the way we react to them.

Accepting responsibility means taking control of your life and the language you use to describe it. As Mitchell says, "It's not what happens to you, it's what you do about it."

QUICK REFERENCE

What you can do right now:
Accept personal responsibility for your present situation and decide to move forward rather than wasting energy by blaming your current condition on past circumstances.

Instead of saying,

"My parents couldn't afford to send me to college like yours did, so I wasn't lucky enough to get a degree. I had to go out and work while you got a free ride in school. Nobody will hire me for a really good job. I can't help it."

Say,

"I haven't gone to college yet, and I have gained a great deal of practical experience in my various jobs. I plan to take night courses and work toward a degree starting this summer. Meanwhile I'm looking into job opportunities that will take advantage of my diverse practical background."

Instead of saying,

"I couldn't meet my quota this month because my car broke down and I just couldn't get to many appointments. It was in the shop for a whole week. It's not my fault. I couldn't help it."

Say,

"I had unexpected car trouble, so I used one full week to telephone all of my longstanding customers whom I haven't talked with in a while. In the long run, I believe this effort will pay off. In the short run, it means I did not make enough appointments to meet my quota this month."

Instead of saying,

"I can't help it; it's someone else's fault."

Say,

"It's my responsibility to change things."

27. You Can Count on Me

It's Saturday morning and you're at your job, working in the Paint Department of a large home-improvement center. A customer calls because his garage-door opener isn't working.

Say out loud to yourself:

"Sorry, I can't help you. The Hardware Department won't be open until 10:00. You'll have to call back later."

Now, say:

"The Hardware Department will be open at 10:00. I'll be happy to help you myself by taking your message and getting it to them. What is your name, please?"

Which sounds like the more responsive, helpful organization? As a customer, which would you rather encounter?

By the eighth ring, I felt impatient. The Marriott organization has a reputation for outstanding service, so I was annoyed when the operator at their Atlanta Marquis property took so long to answer. Finally, after the eleventh ring, an operator answered and transferred me to Reservations. I heard some clicking, and there was silence. I had been cut off!

I called again, waited nine rings, asked for Reservations, heard the clicks and . . . drat!

The third time, my call was answered quickly. Rather than a reservation agent, I asked for the Hotel Manager. The operator placed me on hold while she paged him. After leaving me on "silent hold" a little more than a minute, she came back on the line to tell me he was unavailable. So I said she could transfer me to Reservations. You guessed it. Click.

You've no doubt experienced similar frustrations yourself. Since writing *Phone Power*, I'm on the alert for examples of excellent, as well as poor, handling of phone calls. I often count the rings and time the holds.

On my **fourth** attempt, the operator did connect me with the manager. He listened attentively as I described my experience. When I told him that I wanted to reserve a suite for my family, and was afraid that I would be cut off if I were transferred again, he said,

> **"Mr. Walther, I'm not going to transfer you. I will handle your reservation myself. Then I'll investigate the phone system and find out why you've been getting cut off. When will you be arriving in Atlanta?"**

The manager could have transferred me, and hoped I would be connected smoothly. He could have offered to take my name and number and have someone call me back to take my reservation. But instead he took responsibility and did it himself.

In his best-seller, *Swim With the Sharks Without Being Eaten Alive*, Harvey Mackay identifies many of the phrases that he's used throughout his incredibly successful career. When I interviewed him for *Power Talking*, he said,

"There's a place in this world for anyone who will say, 'I will take care of it.' "

When you deal with people who say, "I will take care of it myself," you know that they are taking personal responsibility for the outcome. That doesn't mean they'll do the tasks themselves, it means they'll be accountable. The hotel's manager didn't walk over to the computer terminal at the Marriott and type in my reservation request. He did personally ensure that it would be handled properly.

QUICK REFERENCE

What you can do right now:
Even though you may not be the person who'll actually perform the tasks, accept personal accountability when you offer to help someone.

Instead of saying,

"I can't help you with that, you'll have to talk with the Customer Service Department."

Say,

"Customer Service can give you the best help with that question, and I'll stay on the line while I transfer you."

Instead of saying,

"Only the Regional Director can authorize a change in the rules. You'll have to call her yourself."

Say,

"The Regional Director has authority in the area you're asking about. I'll be glad to give you that number myself so you can call her directly."

Instead of saying,

"That's not my area. You'll have to get someone else to help you."

Say,

"I'll help you myself by getting your message through to the right department."

28. Do You Choose to Lose?

You work in a position that's well beneath your capabilities. You want time with your family on the weekends, and you don't want to schlep a bulging briefcase home each night. A friend asks why you haven't actively sought career advancement.

Say out loud to yourself:

"I just haven't been able to, what with the family and all. I could be doing a lot more with myself, but unfortunately someone has to be around with the kids on the weekends. Marge doesn't get out much during the week, and she insists on playing tennis every single Saturday. I really don't have much choice."

Now, say:

"I've chosen to dedicate myself to my family right now. I'll concentrate more on my career three or four years from now. Plenty of job opportunities will always be open to me, and now is the only time when I can be with my kids while they're preschoolers. I like giving

Marge some freedom on the weekends. She sure works hard during the week while I'm at the office."

Who's happy? Who thinks of himself as a victim of circumstances?

One of the worst vacations I've ever endured was a two-week holiday in paradise with my family. We stayed at luxurious resorts, the weather was perfect, the beach was ideal. How could it have been so miserable?

My wife has two children from her first marriage, both teenagers. Except during summer vacations and alternating holidays, they live with their dad, so I'm a part-time stepfather. For this trip, we invited each of my stepchildren to bring one of their teenage friends along for two weeks in Hawaii. In addition to the four teenagers, we took our three-month-old infant, Kelcie, who had not yet reached the "sleep-all-night" stage in her development.

The result was that for those two weeks I slept poorly every night. Then I awoke each morning and spent the day reminding four teenagers to close the refrigerator doors after taking out their food, that they should turn off the lights before they go to bed, and so on. Rarely did they heed my instructions.

As the trip progressed, I became more and more grouchy and, in the end, blurted out to my wife that I had never experienced a worse two-week period in my life. I blamed the four teenagers for ruining our trip. The truth is that those four kids are swell young people who behaved well within the bounds of normalcy for thirteen- and fourteen-year-olds. Kelcie is a terrific baby and slept as well as you would expect any three-month-old infant to. Those four teens and a baby did not ruin my vacation. I ruined my vacation.

One challenge I face in writing this book is living up to my own advice. Whenever I complained to my wife about how the kids were wrecking the trip and making me miserable, she reminded me that the decision to enjoy or detest our holiday was completely in my hands. I "chose" to have a bad time. She got even less sleep than I did and was equally inconvenienced by the kids' messiness and lack of consideration. Julie, though, chose to have a good time, and she did.

The children's behaviors were completely predictable. Before ever planning the trip, I could have anticipated what it would be like. When I started feeling resentful, I could have said to myself,

"Four teenagers are not going to be thinking about turning off lights and cleaning their rooms. Our baby will probably wake us up a couple of times every night. I'm going to take those circumstances into account and choose to have a good holiday with my family."

Since I didn't choose to have a good time, the bad time I did have was also my own choice and my responsibility.

One consistent characteristic of winners is that they claim responsibility for their circumstances. They don't play the "victim" role. They don't draw the line at claiming credit and accepting responsibility when things go well. They also embrace the concept of personal responsibility when things aren't perfect. That way they reserve the power to change them.

Powerlessness, the inability to change what you don't like, is a lousy feeling. Ask anyone who's been a hostage in the Middle East or a POW.

Actually, though, there's very little that we can't change. OK, so you're not going to alter the course of a tornado that's bearing down on your home. Those truly unchangeable circumstances, though, are relatively rare.

"There are two big forces at work, external and internal. We have very little control over external forces such as tornadoes, earthquakes, floods, disasters, ill-

ness and pain. What really matters is the internal force. How do I respond to those disasters? Over that I have complete control."

LEO BUSCAGLIA

Winners see the distinction. We've all heard the old prayer:

"God grant me the serenity to accept the things I cannot change, change the things I cannot accept, and the wisdom to know the difference."

The key is in knowing the difference. Most of what most people identify as things they can't change are in fact changeable. And our reactions to the few things that truly can't be changed are, in themselves, matters of choice. I could not change my baby's sleeping patterns, and could not "control" those teenagers and instantly change them into gracious little adults. I could have changed my reaction to the circumstances. I could have **chosen** to enjoy myself despite the kids' behavior.

Recognize that most of what you like and don't like in your life is changeable. And even with the few things that you can't change, you can choose to react positively or negatively. Take responsibility, acknowledge your choices, and use the word **choose** when you describe the situations you're in.

QUICK REFERENCE

What you can do right now:
Avoid "victim" language; acknowledge your responsibility by using the word "choose." When you're unsatisfied with the way things are, choose to change them.

Instead of saying,

"I hate my job, but there's really nothing I can do about it. I'm stuck in this dead-end position, working for a boss I don't really like or respect."

Say,

"For now, I've chosen job security over professional challenge. I could work with more inspiring people, and one day I will. I'm going to start polishing my career skills and check into other opportunities. Meanwhile I'm glad I've created a secure role for myself right here."

Instead of saying,

"Sure, I'd love to get a new car, but we can't afford one. I know it's embarrassing to drive that beat-up junker, but there's just nothing we can do about it."

Say,

"Yes, I'd like a new car, and one day we'll have one. Right now, though, we're making a choice to keep the old one so we can have vacation money and go out for a nice dinner whenever we want to."

Instead of saying,

"I can't change things, I didn't get myself into this fix."

Say,

"I choose to make the best of this situation."

V. Encourage Cooperation and Reduce Conflict

Zig Ziglar says:

> "I believe that you can get everything in life you want if you will just help enough other people get what they want."

Power Talkers are masters at working **with** other people and helping them get what they want. The most successful people are those who ensure that their "partners" also come out ahead.

Power Talkers use their language to encourage cooperation and defuse potential conflicts. They use "win-win" phrasing and form partnerships with others. Their aim is to ensure that both sides in all negotiations win—that there isn't a loser.

One of my consulting clients is a very successful resort developer who has acquired major properties around the country and developed them into profitable condominium and time-share projects. Today Mark is the Director of Marketing for a beautiful resort nestled in the gorgeous countryside near the Wisconsin Dells. Not only has he had a very successful career, he's also guided a whole team of telephone professionals to work together toward impressive mutual successes.

When I asked him what techniques he uses, I heard a lot of Power Talking phrases. He explained that every member of his team starts the year by writing out his or her personal goals, which are reviewed with managers each week. Some new employees have a tendency to write, "Here's what I hope to do," or "Wouldn't it be great if . . ." Mark made it very clear that employees' goals are always rewritten to use the positive expectation language of "I will achieve . . ."

He also pointed out that the goals don't just relate to individuals, they pertain to the organization as a whole, as in, "This is what we will accomplish together." Using Power Talking, conflict-reducing language, is more effective than if he were to gather his employees together and say, "Here's what you have to do to make my resort a success."

In the following chapters you'll meet people who have succeeded in selling ideas and generating cooperation among others, who are good at stimulating group creativity, and who are extraordinarily successful at getting others to do what they want them to do. We are all "salespeople" every day. We "sell" our ideas to others and encourage them to agree.

You'll also learn the techniques employed effectively by talented "peacemakers" whose area of expertise is calming people who have already become upset and hostile. Power Talking leads to increased cooperation and decreased conflict. If you need to work with other people, you'll find these techniques very helpful.

29. Get That "But" Out of Your Mouth!

Your daughter has just passed a proficiency test after completing her first series of computer programming classes. She's working toward a promotion at her company.

Say out loud to yourself:

"You did a good job, Suzanne, **but** you'll need to do more to be ready for that promotion you want."

Now, say this:

"You did a good job, Suzanne, and you'll need to do more to be ready for that promotion you want."

Which sounds more encouraging? Which statement will stimulate Suzanne to move forward in pursuit of her goal?

Every real estate market has its ups and downs, including California's. In the 1980s, Southern California seemed blessed with prosperity. My friend Peter Schweizer and I both invested in California real estate throughout the 80s.

In 1990 Peter came up north to visit me in Seattle. As we walked in the woods, talking about our "California days," he reflected on our properties, saying,

"Yeah, my condo at Mammoth was a good investment, but it's so far away from L.A.; I just don't use it much. You sold your Venice Beach apartment building for a good price, but if you'd only waited another two years, you could've sold it for even more."

Peter still owns his very comfortable condo at a premier California ski resort. He bought it in the early 1980s for less than $20,000. He skis there five or six times a year, often loans it to friends, and also enjoys steady rental income. His investment has paid off superbly, and he could easily sell it for many times his original purchase price.

Yet, as we talked, Peter's concentration was on the negative aspect: "but it's too far away." His attention focused on the phrase following "but."

I am delighted to live in Seattle and I'm glad I moved away from L.A. when I did. My real estate investments in Washington have performed particularly well. Yet, again, Peter's focus was on the negative. The phrase following "but" got the emphasis:

"but . . . you could've sold it for even more."

I may have gotten a better price by selling my California property two years later. However, I wouldn't have been able to buy in Washington just before that market started getting hot.

The effect of the word "but" is to put two viewpoints in opposition to each other and to devalue one of them.

"It was a good investment, **but** . . ."

makes you wonder if it was such a good investment after all.

"You sold at a good price, **but** . . ."

takes away the compliment I was beginning to feel. In the first half of the sentence, my mind heard,

"You did well, George. You have a good sense of timing, anticipated the market well, and made a smart deal."

As soon as **"but"** rolled along, I stepped back and heard,

"Well, maybe you weren't **that** astute. If you'd only waited awhile, you'd have been much smarter."

Peter and I sat down on a boulder overlooking the Seattle skyline and sparkling Puget Sound and I explained that a simple substitution of one word makes a tremendous difference in the impact his statements have on others, and on himself.

> "Yeah, my condo at Mammoth Ski Area was a good investment, **and** it's so far away from L.A. that I don't use it much. You sold your apartment building for a very good price, **and** if you'd waited another two years, you might have sold it for even more."

This way Peter gives himself credit for his good investment sense while recognizing that things have changed. He's no longer interested in driving five hours to his ski condo. Both conditions, the condo being a good investment, **and** his unwillingness to travel five hours to use it, coexist at the same time.

He's also complimenting me on selling my property at a good price **and** acknowledging that the selling price might have been greater had I waited.

The mere substitution of **and** for **but** reduces conflict by suggesting that two ideas can exist at the same time without one overruling the other. Peter's original statement has a much more positive, powerful impact when he uses "and" rather than "but."

Sometimes "but" is what you really mean.

> "It's a very expensive house, but there's no view, the rooms are small, and the school district has a terrible reputation."

Most of the time, though, we say "but" out of habit, when "and" would be a much better choice. Unless you really want to devalue the prior thought ("It's expensive, but a bad value") you're better off substituting the conflict-reducing "and."

When I conduct training sessions for sales professionals, one subject that's often requested is Objection Handling. For example, "What can I do when the customer says, 'But your

price is too high'?" The very first step is to rephrase and repeat the customer's objection using "and" rather than "but."

One of my first sales training clients was Xerox. Their
Business Products Division sells copier paper, toner, and
other supplies. It's common for prospects to point out that
they can buy paper much less expensively if it doesn't carry
the Xerox brand. New salespeople instinctively say.

"It may seem like our paper is more expensive, **but** . . ."

As soon as a salesperson utters "but," the prospect
"hears" him trying to contradict her belief and she stops listening. People don't like to be told they're wrong. They immediately start to resist.

So instead I trained the salespeople to agree with their
prospects:

**"Yes, our paper seems more expensive, and the cost of
making copies includes much more than the paper itself. Cheaper paper, for example, has a tendency to curl
and jam in the machine. That means your expensive
staff resources are pulled away from important projects to clear paper jams."**

The customer isn't being told she's wrong; she's simply
being provided with more complete information on which to
base her buying decisions.

Replacing "but" with "and" creates a more cooperative
atmosphere in sales situations, negotiations, family discus-
sions, and any other time when you want to reduce conflict.
Don't say "but" unless your true intent is to devalue a
thought.

QUICK REFERENCE

What you can do right now:
Make a conscious decision to replace "but" with "and" as

you talk to yourself and to others. Notice that your thinking "opens up" as ideas coexist instead of conflict.

Instead of saying,

"I'm getting the hang of my new job, but there are a few things I don't really understand."

Say instead,

"I'm getting the hang of my new job, and there are a few things I don't really understand."

Instead of saying,

"I know you want to expand the sales meeting to three full days, **but** consider the budget impact."

Say instead,

"I know you want to expand the sales meeting to three full days, and consider the budget impact."

Instead of saying,

"I can see that it's a good product, **but** it's expensive."

Say instead,

"I can see that it's a good product, and it's expensive."

30. Let's Do It!

During a brainstorming/feedback session with your sales team, it becomes clear that there are several sore points the group is concerned about. One member complains that supervisors in her department ring a bell when incoming calls are backed up, and she finds it distracting. She suggests eliminating the bell.

Say out loud to yourself:

"Well, I'm sorry you don't like hearing it, but it's the only way supervisors can let everyone know that it's time to get back to work. Without the bell, they'd have to constantly walk around gathering up their people. It's the only practical way to do it."

Now, say:

"I can understand how that would be distracting. Let's find another way to let everyone know when the department is very busy. How about a series of lights up on the wall? If the bell hurts more than it helps, we'll experiment with other techniques."

Which sounds like the reaction that will encourage more brainstorming ideas, quite possibly leading to innovative breakthroughs? Which will "shut down" the participants' creative thinking?

Market researchers often use "Focus Groups" to sample customers' feelings about a company's products and services. A dozen or so customers are invited to an informal discussion in a research company's facility and are observed through a one-way mirror. They're told up front that company representatives will be watching them, and they're encouraged to say whatever they have on their mind. A moderator gently guides the discussion, carefully holding back any of his own opinions to avoid influencing the participants' views.

Right after I completed my graduate studies, I was employed by a major advertising agency as an Account Executive. I handled several multimillion-dollar accounts, including Continental Airlines, McCulloch Chain Saws, and Van de Kamp frozen foods. Hearing what customers really thought about our ads and the clients' products in Focus Group sessions was often very revealing. (It was kind of fun playing peeping Tom behind that mirror, too.)

Recently, Stew Leonard, owner of the world's largest grocery store, told me about a Focus Group session involving several of his store managers interacting with 16 women who had been asked to talk about buying fish.

One woman in the group said,

"I won't buy fish from your store because I only buy fresh fish, and yours isn't."

The Fish Department manager shot to his feet and responded,

"What do you mean it's not fresh? I handle the purchasing myself. We buy fresh fish every single day at Fulton Market."

The woman responded,

"If that were true, then why would you put it in those plastic packages like the frozen fish at the supermarket? I like to buy my fish nice and fresh, right off the ice."

The store was already selling 15,000 pounds of fresh fish every week, so it would have been understandable if the fish buyer had set out to convince the woman that she was wrong. Instead, Stew said,

So she likes her fish on ice. If she thinks it makes such a big difference, let's do it."

The very next day, store personnel began building a fish display with a bed of ice. The week after installing the "fish bar," sales doubled! The interesting thing is that sales of the regular packaged fish did not decline at all. The extra 15,000 pounds of fish sold each week was all new sales, apparently purchased by customers who shared that woman's feelings.

It would have been very easy to be closed-minded about the fish situation—and lose out on more than three-quarters of a million pounds of fish sales each year.

Power Talkers definitely have strong opinions and aren't afraid to express them—when appropriate. Convincing the other person that your point of view is right can sometimes help you win the battle but lose the war. As a Power Talker, you want to make other people feel comfortable about expressing their ideas and encourage them to think creatively. Only after evaluating the merits of various approaches can you determine the best course to follow.

One of my clients in the resort development business has been very successful selling memberships in a national network of private campgrounds. For them, as for most sales organizations, new sales prospects who are referred by existing customers have the very best potential for becoming satisfied customers. The cost of finding them is low, their conversion rate is high, and they tend to be happier with their purchases than are other nonreferral new customers. Referred prospects have already been influenced by the most powerful form of advertising, word-of-mouth publicity from a satisfied customer.

I observed as my client gathered her employees together and presented them with the goal of brainstorming a dozen new ways to increase the flow of referrals. She didn't promote her own ideas and she didn't criticize any of the suggestions. In less than 30 minutes, the team had come up with 15 excellent approaches.

This manager was a conscientious user of Power Talking language, an encouraging cheerleader rather than a domineering critic. Her role was to keep saying, "That's good. I like it. Let's do it. Wow, that can work. Let's get some more ideas. Keep 'em coming. Who sees a way to connect these two?"

And when someone else in the group pooh-poohed an idea, she reminded them to keep an open mind.

Encourage other people to cooperate by inviting their input and ideas. Welcome unusual suggestions rather than quashing them. Get all involved parties to throw their ideas out on the table so creative solutions can result.

QUICK REFERENCE

What you can do right now:
Whenever you seek others' input and suggestions, stimulate a free flow of ideas, no matter how crazy some might seem.
Instead of saying,

"I want to give everyone a chance to suggest one or two approaches on this project. Please keep our limited budget in mind."

Say,

"Let's get lots of ideas going. Don't worry about how much they may cost. We'll consider practicality later. For now, anything goes."

Instead of saying,

"Your suggestion just won't work. Believe me, I've personally seen it fail at two other companies."

Say,

"Good suggestion. Let's keep going and come up with some more."

Instead of saying,

"That's not practical, it'll never work."

Say,

"That's an unusual approach, let's go with it and see where we end up."

31. Do ME a Favor for a Change

A fund-raiser for your local PBS station phones you at home. After introducing himself, he explains that he's hoping you'll make a donation.

Say out loud to yourself:

"I was wondering if you could do me a favor and make a contribution to the station. We have this contest going on for the phone reps, and I'm really close to winning a Disneyland trip for my family."

Now, say:

"We want to continue offering fine educational programming for you and your family. With your contribution, you'll receive our informative monthly newsletter and, of course, you'll have the good feeling of knowing that you're helping to provide your family with quality television programs."

Which approach will motivate you to open your checkbook?

There are lots of reasons that motivate people to do business together. Often, they're selfish ones. These can be

counterproductive when it comes to encouraging cooperation. Only one reason really counts: The other guy must believe that he'll be better off by doing what you suggest.

I'm surely not against helping out a friend. When it comes
to a business proposition, though, there's only one party I'm
really watching out for: ME! It's amazing how many salespeople tend to concentrate on why **they'll** be better off if
they get you to buy something. As a customer, it's completely irrelevant to me—unless we have a friendship—that
you're "just this close" to meeting your quota for the month,
or about to qualify for some kind of prize.

When I began presenting sales seminars in the early
1980s, many sales trainers used a popular acronym: WIIFM.
The explanation went like this:

> "Whenever you're scripting a sales presentation, design-
> ing an ad, or writing copy for a direct mail campaign, only
> one thing matters: WIIFM! *What's In It For Me*? That's
> what customers want to know; that's what they're asking
> themselves as you present your case for what you want
> them to do. They don't care about a salesperson's com-
> pany, product features, or personal situation. They care
> only about themselves. They want to know how the action
> you're suggesting will make them be better off."

A hospital information operator in one of my seminar audiences recently asked me a question following my presentation.

She said,

> *"When I ask callers for their insurance information, they
> often get huffy and indignant. Some of them don't have in-
> surance, and I think they're afraid I won't help them if I
> find that out. When I tell them I have to get the informa-
> tion for our internal call reporting statistics, they still
> seem uncooperative. What can I say to make them feel like
> cooperating?"*

I wanted to help her figure that answer out for herself, so I just stood there with my arms crossed and said,

"Why should I want to give you my insurance information?"

She seemed confused, and didn't immediately recognize that I was role-playing with her and taking the stance that her callers adopted. I continued,

*"I don't care about **your** statistical project or your hospital's requirements. Just tell me why **I** should want to give you the information."*

She caught on. My point was that she should assume that any caller is constantly asking himself, "What's In It For Me?"

It took her only a few seconds to come up with the caller-oriented benefit:

"Once I know a little about your insurance coverage, I can make sure I'm referring you to the best medical option for your circumstances. If you don't have insurance, I can make arrangements to talk with a public health facility. And if you do, I can determine which of our physicians already use direct billing plans with your particular insurance carrier, and that can make things much simpler for you when it comes to minimizing paperwork."

She got it! Her callers don't care about the hospital at all. They only care about themselves. She was really setting out to "sell" them on the value of cooperating with her information request.

Now when she wants to get insurance information from a caller, she can "sell" them on the benefits of cooperating with her question by saying,

"In order to make sure I'm referring you to the physician or facility that's best for your situation, please tell

me who your insurance carrier is. That way if one of the hospital's doctors has a direct billing arrangement with your company, your paperwork will be minimized later on."

When you want someone to cooperate, to follow your lead, to do something for you, take off your shoes. Get in the other guy's shoes. Look at the scenario from his standpoint and show him how he'll benefit by taking the action you recommend.

QUICK REFERENCE

What you can do right now:
When you need someone's cooperation, figure out why his participation will benefit *him*, not *you*. Emphasize the benefits he'll realize by following your suggestion.

Instead of saying,

"My son's Boy Scout troop is selling firewood, and if you could just do me a favor and buy two or three sacks, he'll be able to go on the campout next month."

Say,

"My son's Boy Scout troop is selling firewood, and it's an excellent value. The price is right, and you'll find it's good, long-burning hardwood. How much would you like to buy?"

Instead of saying,

"Look, when you interrupt me several times a day with your questions, it's almost impossible for me to get any serious work done. Would you do me a favor and save them up so I don't have to keep breaking my concentration?"

Say,

"You deserve my full attention when I'm answering your questions. The best way to get it would be to meet with me once or twice a day. That way I'll be able to really concentrate on helping you and cover several questions in depth each time."

Instead of saying,

"Will you do me a favor?"

Say,

"Here's why this will be good for you."

32. You Get What You Ask For

You meet with an important customer because you've heard that he's been talking to one of your competitors. Fearing that you could be about to lose his business, you decide to find out if there's something he's unhappy about.

Say out loud to yourself:

"John, you've been happy with our service, haven't you?"

Now, say:

"John, you're a very important customer and my aim is to constantly improve the way we serve you. What two or three areas would you like us to improve upon?"

Which question will encourage your customer to provide

complete, candid feedback? Which will open a dialogue that leads toward a stronger relationship?

"Hello, Mr. Walther, this is Debra in Room Service. I'm calling to find out if you were pleased with the pizza we delivered to your room this evening."

Nobody from any hotel's Room Service department had ever called me before. Debra asked if my pizza had been warm enough, spiced about right, and delivered on time. I answered that it had been fine. I was surprised at her call and wondered if she had some ulterior motive. Was there some sort of pizza recall? I dismissed the call, got some sleep, and presented my first training seminar for Ford Motor Credit the next morning.

The following month I returned to present another seminar for Ford and again stayed at the same hotel. I rarely leave my room the evening before a presentation. Most of the time I order from Room Service, review my program notes, and get to bed early so I'm fresh for my audience the next morning. I ordered the local chicken dish and enjoyed it. Once again my phone rang after finishing my meal.

"Good evening, Mr. Walther, this is Debra calling from Room Service. I'd like to find out if your chicken was prepared to your liking."

The same young woman had called again. I answered her questions and asked her a few myself. I wanted to know more about why she was calling. Debra explained that she calls every single guest half an hour after their Room Service meals are delivered to ensure that things were just right.

I was struck with the simplicity of her approach. Of course! If you want to find out how to improve Room Service, or any other service, the best thing to do is ask your guest or customer directly. Very few people take the time to fill out those "guest comment cards" propped up on most hotels' bedside tables. But if you phone guests in their rooms, they'll probably talk to you.

By the time I'd presented my seventh training seminar for Ford, Debra and I had become quite friendly. I autographed a copy of *Phone Power* and delivered it to her office so I could observe her in action as she made her calls soliciting guest feedback. Later that evening I listened for two hours in her dingy cubicle right by the service elevators in the sub-basement, where the hotel's kitchen is situated.

Think of all the times you've been served an overpriced, mediocre meal in a restaurant and commented to your companions that the service was poor to boot. Invariably, when the maître d' asks, "Was everything satisfactory? You enjoyed your meal?" you smile and say, "Oh yes, thank you, it was fine." Why didn't you tell him the truth? Perhaps you could sense that he didn't really want to know. His question was a habitual routine—a hollow nicety.

As I sat beside Debra and listened in on her calls that evening, I noticed that guests were all quite surprised to hear from her, yet very few offered any really helpful suggestions. Were they really 100% satisfied, or did Debra's questions themselves need improving?

Most calls went about like this:

"Hello, Mrs. Hightsman, this is Debra in Room Service. I'm calling to find out if you were satisfied with the soup and salad we delivered to your room earlier this evening. Was everything OK?"

The guests nearly always said something like this:

"Well, how nice of you to ask! Yes, everything was fine. Thanks for calling."

After hearing several of these brief conversations, I asked Debra,

"Do you really just want to know if they were satisfied? Or are you looking for suggestions to help you improve? If you want more helpful feedback, let's ask a question that gets at the heart of what you're after. Instead of asking IF THEY ARE HAPPY, let's ask guests HOW WE CAN MAKE THEM HAPPIER. If we've already made them as happy as they can possibly be, they'll say so."

So, on the next call, Debra changed her question:

"Good evening, Mr. Blackstone. This is Debra calling from Room Service. I hope you enjoyed the prime rib dinner we delivered to you tonight. I'd like to find out what one aspect of your meal could have been a little nicer."

This took Mr. Blackstone by surprise.

"Oh, my, it was very nice. Let's see, how could it have been a little better? Well, the entrée was just right, but I noticed that my dinner roll was rather hard. You could check up on the freshness. It's just a small thing. Everything else was fine."

Debra zeroed in on the dinner rolls, and other guests reported that theirs were also a little stale. She contacted the bakery chef, arranged for a new batch, and continued with her calls to help her hotel set the pace for constantly improving its service.

The best way to reinforce and improve any relationship is to stop and take stock. Whether it's with a customer, a colleague, a spouse, or a friend, find out exactly where you stand and make improvements where needed. When you want to improve any kind of relationship, you must take the time to ask for sincere, candid, complete feedback about how you can make things better.

Frequently, feedback comes your way without even asking for it. It may be of a critical nature, and may be couched in harsh terms. When you hear criticism, it's important to immediately let the other party know that you welcome the comments. That doesn't mean that you will necessarily agree with them or find them valid. The important thing is to keep the communication channels open and show the other person that you respect his viewpoint.

I recommend a two-step dialogue. First, say something like,

"I'm really glad you're telling me this, and I do want to know how you feel. Thanks for being comfortable enough to tell me what's on your mind."

Then follow up by asking for specifics. Don't dismiss the criticism after hearing the generalities. Instead ask for more.

"Please help me understand why you feel that way. What did I do to cause your reaction? I want to be able to watch for it myself in the future."

Customer service mavens, employee productivity counselors, and family therapists constantly remind us to ask how we can improve our relationships. That's good advice. **How you ask** is almost as important as asking. Presume that you could do a better job in some area of your relationship and then ask exactly what that area is. Don't ask if things are OK; ask how you can make them better.

QUICK REFERENCE

What you can do right now:
Make it a habit to ask at least one relationship-improving question every single day.

Instead of saying,

"Are you feeling pretty good about our marriage these days?"

Say,

"What's one thing I can focus on to be a better marriage partner for you?"

Instead of saying,

"Are you happy with our service?"

Say,

"How could we improve our service for you?"

Instead of saying,

"Have you been pleased with my accomplishments since you promoted me?"

Say,

"I feel good about my accomplishments since my promotion, and I want to do even better. What are two or three things I can focus on to exceed your expectations?"

Instead of saying,

"Was everything satisfactory?"

Say,

"How can I do a better job for you?"

33. So, What CAN You Do?

You work at an airline ticket counter. An upset woman approaches and explains that she is on her way to visit an ailing grandparent but has lost her ticket. She asks you for a refund.
Say out loud to yourself:

"No, I can't issue you a refund for the ticket. You'll just have to fill out a lost ticket application and wait. You probably won't get an answer for three to four weeks."

Now, say:

"What I can do is issue a new replacement ticket and charge it to your credit card. Then I'll help you with the lost ticket application and forward it to our research department."

Which approach is likely to make your agitated passenger feel that you are working cooperatively toward a positive solution? Which will make her feel even more upset?

One morning while my wife and I were visiting a resort, we decided to have lunch a little early and headed down to the poolside terrace restaurant shortly before noon. The place was empty. No one else was seated, and a busboy was arranging silverware on the tables. The hostess saw us waiting at the entryway and approached with a smile, saying, "We'll be open and ready to begin serving lunch in just a few minutes. I can seat you then."

The first thing that ran through my mind was, "If you're going to be open in just a few minutes, why don't you just let us go in and sit down at one of those empty tables and wait?" I probably would have argued the point with her had she used the approach I'm more used to hearing: "The restaurant is closed now and we won't be open for a while. I can't seat you until then."

What she said carried the exact same meaning as the more common negative version. Her approach, though, informed us in a completely positive manner, stressing what she **could** do rather than what she couldn't. Instead of arguing or creating a conflict, Julie and I went to wait in the lounge and enjoy a drink. A few other couples had been greeted with her smile and positive statement, and they had also headed for the lounge to enjoy tropical drinks. That one hostess had used Power Talking—a positive rephrasing of a negative statement. The end result was that we were all happy to wait, her busboys and other staff members were able to prepare for lunch without interference, and the bar did some extra business!

For every "can't" statement, there's a "can." The negative "can't" version immediately erects a roadblock and creates a conflict with the listener. Compare the effect of "We won't be open this weekend and I'm afraid I can't get your order ready until Monday afternoon" with "We will be open again on Monday and I'll be glad to have your order ready that afternoon." The positive version is easier to understand. It also projects a much more friendly, cooperative, helpful impression.

I noticed how a flight attendant described entree choices on a recent flight to Chicago. To passengers in the front of the cabin, he offered lasagna, chicken, and beef tips. When he reached my row, the beef was gone. He said,

> **"Mr. Walther, I can offer you the lasagna entree, which gets lots of compliments, or the chicken dish, which I particularly like myself. Which do you prefer?"**

What he didn't say is, "Oh, I'm so sorry, we're all out of beef, I can't offer that to you." By positively describing the alternatives he *did* have available, I felt happy about the choices.

Always choose to use the positive version of a negative

statement. Tell people what you *can* do, not what you *can't*. They'll understand you more easily and feel better about what you've told them.

QUICK REFERENCE

What you can do right now:
Whenever you start telling someone what you can't do, change your focus and substitute a statement indicating what you can do.

Instead of saying,

> "I can't give you a riverview room tonight; I'll have to put you in a city view for tonight and move you tomorrow."

Say,

> **"I can give you a city view room tonight and then have you moved into a riverview room tomorrow. That way you'll get to enjoy both views."**

Instead of saying,

> "I can't answer that question for you myself. I'll have to go check with one of our customer service people and get back to you later."

Say,

> **"I can help you with that question by talking to our customer service department and getting a definite answer. I'll contact you this afternoon to let you know exactly where things stand. What time would you like me to call?"**

Instead of saying,

> "Here's what I can't do."

Say,

"Here's what I can do."

34. Breaking the Language
Barrier

One of your customers is very upset about a recent order. In a highly emotional state, he calls you and starts spouting off.
Say out loud to yourself:

"Well, Chris, it looks like you have a problem. What do you expect me to do about it?"

Now, say this:

"Chris, it's clear that we have a challenge here. Let's work together and solve it."

Which approach is likely to move you toward a solution and create a cooperative atmosphere with Chris?

Part of my training work involves showing organizations how they can do a much better job when dealing with upset customers. One of my assignments involved the elite team of US WEST Cellular's Customer Service representatives known as the Retention Group. Their job is to "save" customers who are so unhappy that they've threatened to cancel their cellular phone accounts. I "met" Chris B. on my first day of monitoring calls with my new client.
Everyone in the Customer Service Call Center had either been yelled at by Chris B. or had heard animated stories

about his tantrums, demands, and verbal abuse. Almost everyone hoped to avoid handling Chris's calls because he was totally unreasonable.

Then along came Mary Hatcher. Her tone of voice, demeanor, and superb language skills reassure you that everything's going to be OK. Mary makes things right.

By the time his call was transferred to Mary, Chris B. had already been complaining (vigorously!) for two years about US WEST Cellular's service. She'd heard plenty of stories about him and decided to make him her "special person." Mary determined that one of her professional challenges would be to turn this irascible customer around.

The first time Chris was transferred to her, Mary got personal:

> **"Chris, I'm familiar with your situation, and I am going to help you. Here's what I've been wondering: How could our service be so horrible, and yet you still keep doing business with us? Perhaps there's something else that you feel unhappy about. If you're having troubles in other areas, the last thing I want to do is contribute to your discomfort."**

He was taken by surprise. She had immediately cut through the usual business façade to uncover the root of the problem.

Chris opened up and explained that his business life was a mess. He had problems in his relationships with employees. He wasn't getting along with his partner. Chris was doing poorly on many fronts. His favorite outlet was his car phone, where he could call Customer Service and unleash a toll-free tirade at someone he'd never have to face.

Chris was a specialist at erecting dividing barriers. His approach was:

> *"I'm the poor mistreated customer, you're the big rich company making money off me, and you don't understand*

*what it's like to be on my side of the table. What are you
gonna do to make up for my mistreatment?"*

Mary is a specialist at dissolving barriers. Her approach is
to get on the customer's side. In fact, she describes her position as being a Customer Advocate. Her language is filled
with impediment-dissolving, team-building phrases.

**"We do have an uncomfortable situation here. Let's
work together and solve this."**

Instead of permitting a verbal barrier to separate her from
the customer, she dissolves it. Rather than trying to convince
the customer he's wrong, she validates his feelings and
moves ahead.

**"I understand why you feel that way. You have a right
to expect superior service. Let's find out what's going
on so we can fix it."**

Mary's approach works. With her words alone, she
showed Chris B. that there was no barrier dividing them. She
aligned with him, on his side, and he calmed down. Other
Customer Service reps started reporting that he was actually
sounding nicer when he called them. Mary succeeded in
turning Chris B. around by deciding to dissolve the barrier
that he imagined was dividing them.

Most conflict situations involve imagined barriers. When
people are working together, on the same side of the table,
there's no confrontation. The first challenge in reducing conflicts is to dissolve those barriers. You must show you aim to
be a partner, not an adversary.

Be careful to avoid pronouns that contribute to the me/you
schism. Use "we" and "us" rather than "you" and "I" to
show that you view your relationship as a partnership.

Be sure to point out any common ground you share with
your counterpart. Help the other person see that you truly are

empathetic. Once you establish common ground with someone, they're much more likely to treat you as a problem-solving partner instead of an adversary.

Peacemakers like Mary Hatcher are masters at using conflict-reducing language. The principles they use are easy to master, and you'll most likely have an opportunity to use them today. Use words that show your counterpart that you want to dissolve barriers and work together.

QUICK REFERENCE

What you can do right now:
When you're involved in a conflict, use your language to show that you're intent on working **with**, not **against** the other person; show that you and your counterpart are on the same side of the table.

Instead of saying,

"It's your problem, what do you expect me to do about it?"

Say,

"We share this challenge, let's solve it together."

Instead of saying,

"Here's what you'll have to do."

Say,

"Here's what we can do."

Instead of saying,

"I understand what you want. But I must adhere to my policies."

Say,

"We share some important common goals. Let's see how we can work together."

35. You're Invited!

A group of neighbors has decided to contest a local landfill operator's request to extend his operating permit and triple the site size. You want the dump closed. It's going to take money. Your neighborhood association meets to decide how you will proceed.

Say out loud to yourself:

"This is going to cost a lot of money and you'll all have to make donations. You're also going to have to get others in the neighborhood to contribute, too, unless you can come up with a better idea."

Now, say:

"We're going to need a lot of money to succeed. We can ask everyone for cash contributions or we can hold some kind of fund-raising event like a big garage sale and invite the whole neighborhood to participate. Or we can do something else altogether. What are some other approaches we can consider?"

Which sounds like the tactic that will generate the most cooperation? Which is almost sure to fail?

One challenge I regularly face as a speaker is getting my audience back in the room after each coffee break. Typically, the seminar organizer or the client's Meeting Planner schedules 15 minutes for coffee at some point during the program. This usually drags out to 25 or 30 minutes, until I remind the client that we have a lot of ground to cover and suggest that he reassemble the audience.

Then the Meeting Planner goes into the foyer, where everyone is munching sweet rolls and guzzling coffee. He tries unsuccessfully to get the crowd moving back in, and finally stands on a chair and shouts, "We're running late. You'll have to return to your seats now."

I've found a much more effective Power Talking approach. Just before it's time to begin a break, I say to my audience:

> **"Everything is set for our coffee break now, and I'd like you to decide how we'll handle it. We can make it a long break that drags out to 25 or 30 minutes, or we can get right back to these Power Talking techniques and resume our program in exactly 15 minutes. Please raise your hand if you prefer . . ."**

My audiences always choose the shorter break. They didn't come to drink coffee; they want ideas and strategies that they'll be able to put to work—and benefit from—right away. I also make a point of saying, "My watch reads 12 minutes past 10:00 right now, so we'll start again at 10:27. Enjoy the refreshments, and we'll resume at 10:27." (My experience has shown that for some reason people pay more attention to odd times. If you schedule a meeting to resume at 10:27, you'll have more people there on time than if you schedule it for 10:30.)

Still, human nature seems to include a herding instinct. Everybody waits for someone else to start moving back into the presentation room. At my seminars I've found that I'm the best person to play that role. At about 10:25 I move out to the foyer and start the herd moving. Instead of calling out, I approach four or five different clusters of people who are talking to each other and say, "I invite you to bring your coffee back into the ballroom; we're just about to resume."

There are two key elements of my audience-assembling technique that make it effective. First, the participants "own" their course of action. I don't dictate what they'll do, I let them choose. Second, I consciously use the word "invite." Nobody likes orders or mandates. Everyone likes an invitation. If I were using the more common audience reassembling techniques, people would be thinking,

"Oh, gee, do we have to go back in already?"

Instead, these same people look back at me and say,

"Oh, how nice. An invitation. We accept!"

This approach works every time. After all, the audience did come to get as many ideas as possible. I'm using Power Talking techniques to help ensure that they get maximum value from the program.

Think of the situations you face in your work and daily life. When you want to encourage cooperation, give the other person a role in choosing among options, and then "invite" him or her to follow through.

Isn't it odd that we so often use the phrase "have to" when we're inviting somebody to cooperate with us? Those words suggest that the other person has no choice, that the action we're about to describe is mandatory and quite possibly unpleasant.

Friends of ours recently said,

"You'll have to come over for dinner sometime soon."

We like them, and do want to join them, but it sounded more like a command than a gracious invitation. Soon after, I caught myself saying to other friends,

"We'll have to get together one of these weekends."

There again, an indication that socializing is more of an unwanted obligation than a preference. It's a lot more inviting to say,

> **"We'd like to get together with you next week. How 'bout going out for a movie and late dinner on Friday or brunch at our place on Sunday?"**

To encourage cooperation, don't mandate that people do what you want them to. Invite them to choose among options, so they "own" their preference.

QUICK REFERENCE

What you can do right now:
When you want others to cooperate with you, "invite" them to do so and give them a choice about what they'll do.
Instead of saying,

> "To be considered, you'll have to take this form, fill it out completely, and then bring it back in the morning."

Say,

> **"You can take this form home overnight and complete it at your convenience. Then I invite you to come back and drop it off in the morning."**

Instead of saying,

> "You'll have to send the whole unit back to the Regional Service Center to get it repaired."

Say,

> **"You can either send the unit to the Regional Service Center or take it to a dealer. Which is more convenient for you?"**

Instead of saying,

"Here's what you'll have to do."

Say,

"I invite you to choose the approach that will work best for you."

36. I Recommend

You sell life insurance and are talking with a young couple about their needs. Their first child is due in a few months, and the husband plans to buy a substantial term-life policy. You believe that he should also carry a term policy on his wife.

Say out loud to yourself:

"One other thing you might possibly want to consider is buying a policy to cover your wife. Although her health is excellent right now, you never know what might happen to her during childbirth."

Now, say:

"It's wise of you to provide protection in case you personally aren't able to generate income for your family. Considering the possibility of complications during childbirth, I recommend that you secure temporary protection covering your wife as well."

Which approach is more likely to catch your prospective customer's interest and show that you are genuinely concerned for his welfare? Which is more likely to result in a sale?

That was no hypothetical example; it's exactly what my insurance agent said to me when I recently bought my first insurance policy. I'd always been dead set against buying insurance—until we learned that our first child was on the way.

When I was a kid, my dad offered simple advice (to anyone who'd listen) for dealing with life insurance salespeople. He'd say,

". . . and I always tell them I'll buy whatever they suggest, in the amount they think is best, so long as they pay every single premium, including their own commissions."

After hearing Dad often repeat his "funny" strategy at dinner gatherings as part of his party repertoire, I learned a clear—and erroneous—lesson about life insurance salespeople: "Don't ever buy anything from them. They're just after commissions."

I felt a lot different when Julie and I found that we were about to become parents. I decided it was finally time for me to have insurance protection for her and our baby. I reluctantly made the big jump and actually asked for an appointment with a life insurance salesman! I hadn't considered buying a policy for Julie, too, but did so after hearing the salesman's recommendation.

After buying the two policies, we decided to have our yard landscaped to include a nice play area for the baby. The salesman, after "closing" our landscaping sale, said,

"It's a very small additional investment, and I do recommend that you have us install landscape fabric underneath the ground-cover plantings and decorative mulch. That will prevent 95% of all weeds and will make sure that you're able to enjoy this landscaping without having to pull weeds every weekend."

We bought the landscaping fabric.

My life insurance salesman and the landscaper both used a common approach: They "recommended" a course of action.

"Recommend" is an amazingly powerful word. Whatever your occupation, you sell ideas to others all day long. Whenever you're selling, make strong use of the word "recommend."

I was hired to train a group of sales professionals at Resort Condominiums International in Indianapolis, a company that arranges for time-share vacation exchanges. One of their goals was to encourage callers to renew their memberships early and for longer terms. As I began the training sessions, I noticed that the phone reps commonly used an approach like:

> "Oh, and say, incidentally, while I've got you on the line, I notice that your membership will be expiring in another few months, so you might want to start thinking about getting that renewed. And while you're at it, one thing you might possibly want to consider is the cost savings from getting a three- or five-year extension instead of just a single year. Would that perhaps be of interest to you?"

I urged them to stop being so tentative and instead use the C.P.R. sales formula, a sales-closing technique I wrote about in *Phone Power*. Many readers have reported that it works wonderfully and helps them establish positive relationships with their customers.

First, *C*onsult with the customer and ask about his future plans. Does he enjoy using his exchange privileges? Does he have lifetime ownership of his time-share condo? Does he like to cut down on paperwork and save money?

Next, the reps *P*ersonalize the benefits of a multiyear renewal for that individual caller. They show the member that, considering his personal situation and interests, a multiyear renewal is a better way to go.

Finally, the rep uses the word *R*ecommend to "close the sale."

> **"Mr. Volwiler, in your situation I recommend the five-year renewal plan. You mentioned that you do plan to continue using your exchange privileges, and that you don't want to be bothered with the annual mailings and calls reminding you that your membership is about to expire. With the five-year plan, you'll be renewed, with exchange privileges, for five full years. There's no annual paperwork to bother with and you can't possibly forget to renew each year. I recommend that we put that through now. Which credit card shall I charge it on for you?"**

Soon after the training session, one of the R.C.I. telephone reps called my office and exclaimed,

> *"It works! It's magic. I've been making sure I say 'recommend' in every call, and my sales closing rate is up by 25%."*

"Recommend" isn't magic. And it does work. It works because it's a behavioral trigger. In the case of a salesperson, it's easy to get off track and focus on your own needs rather than the customers'. You may start thinking about the sales contest, your product training, your commission checks, and everything except what matters most: your customers' needs.

Using the word "recommend" reminds salespeople that their role is to act as the customers' partner. The R.C.I. rep's success didn't stem from his use of a magic word. It was a result of focusing on the customer, asking about his needs, and matching them with the benefits of R.C.I.'s long-term renewal plan by recommending.

Make "Recommend" an important part of your closing argument when selling a product, service, or idea. By practicing the C.P.R. approach and emphasizing the "recommend" step, you will be putting your concentration right where it belongs: on the other person's welfare.

QUICK REFERENCE

What you can do right now:
Whenever you set out to "sell" an idea, service, or product, focus on the benefits to the other person and use the word "recommend" to close the sale.

Instead of saying,

"Would you be interested in renewing?"

Say,

"Based on what you've told me, I recommend that you renew now and avoid the September 15 dues increase."

Instead of saying,

"I want to sell you . . ."

Say,

"I recommend that you purchase . . ."

Instead of saying,

"One thing you might possibly want to consider is to . . ."

Say,

"I recommend that you . . ."

37. What Sounds Fair to You?

Your neighbor has two large cedar trees on his side of the property line that separates your two houses. One tree looks like it's dying. Since it provides privacy for your deck, you want to keep it alive. He's shown little interest in taking action, so you call in a tree service and are told that a deep-root fertilizer injection will cost $150. You think your neighbor should pay, since it's his tree.

Say out loud to yourself:

"Look, you don't seem to care much about saving your cedar tree. It's pretty obvious that it's about to die. I called a tree service to get their advice. They say it'll cost $150 to fertilize it and I think you should take responsibility to keep it alive."

Now, say:

"I've noticed that the big cedar tree isn't doing very well. I know you're busy, so when I saw all the brown needles, I went ahead and called in a tree surgeon to find out if it can be saved. They say it'll cost about $150. The tree is on your property and we both benefit from the privacy it provides. What do you think would be a fair way to handle the expense?"

Which sounds like the approach that will promote a favorable outcome you're both going to be happy about? Which will make your neighbor think about putting up a tall fence and suggesting that you keep your nose on your own side of it?

Donna, a manager at a well-known Japanese office copier company, called my office to inquire about purchasing *Phone Power* audio and video tapes for all of her dealers.

She wanted to help the independent retailers use effective telemarketing to sell copiers and supplies. This is an excellent strategy for many companies that rely on a network of independent dealers and distributors. When you help your dealers become more profitable, they buy more of your products as they succeed and their business grows.

From our first phone conversation, I felt that Donna would be difficult to deal with. She was intent on getting a special price on everything. I respect people who want to get the best possible value, but in her case there was something overly pushy about her approach. I explained that she would receive a 30% discount if her order totaled 250 or more individual tapes. She wanted 225, which qualified her for a 25% discount. She eventually placed an order for 250 items. I felt confident sending her the tapes along with an invoice, since the company is a very large and reputable one.

Three months later the invoice remained unpaid, though Donna had advised me repeatedly that it was "in the process" of being handled. Then along came a box containing 25 of the tapes. Her handwritten note said,

"I'm returning these 25 tapes for credit. Please reissue the invoice and it will be paid promptly."

My first reaction was to think to myself:

"What a con. She really only wanted 225 in the first place. She sat on the bill for three months, sent back the 25 that had qualified her for the lower price break, and now she expects me to give her a full credit for them so she'll still get the 30% discount on her 225. She's not going to get away with this!"

Here I was, getting all worked up over her attempt to take advantage of me. I thought of writing a "What kind of fool do you think I am?" letter. Then I thought of confronting her on the phone and telling her she wouldn't get away with her cheap tricks. And then I stopped for a minute and calmed down. The total amount of money at stake was a little less than $200. And I didn't really know that she wanted to take advantage of me, I just assumed it based on my reading of her personality.

I realized that the $200 wasn't my concern, I just wanted to be treated fairly. She was holding all the cards, though, since she hadn't yet paid a cent. Was the extra money my top priority? No. My real objectives were to: (1) Feel good about the transaction, (2) Keep the door open for a future relationship with the company, and (3) Get paid. All of those objectives were contingent upon her feeling good about working with me. Rather than writing a nasty letter or having a telephone confrontation, I decided to use a Power Talking approach. In situations like this one, good questions get you a lot further than strong statements.

I called Donna the next morning and said:

"Hello, Donna. I got the 25 tapes you sent back. Thanks for packing them up so carefully. They were in fine condition. I also got your note asking for a corrected invoice. I'd like your advice. Your original invoice included a 30% discount, based on 250 tapes. If you had ordered only 225 in the first place, you would have earned a 25% discount. I don't charge any restocking fee or other penalty for handling your return, and I have been waiting for three months to get your payment. Please tell me what you think would be the fairest way to handle this."

Presented with these facts, she considered for a moment and said,

"Well, I'd like the 30% discount, of course, but I guess the fairest thing would be for you to re-invoice me at the 25% discount."

If she had insisted that the 30% discount was fair, I would have issued the new invoice without quibbling. As it was, I sent her a bonus gift with her invoice since I felt good about working with her.

The point is this: Almost everyone will treat you fairly if you give them a chance. Power Talkers keep the big picture, long-run view in mind. They don't sweat that small stuff. They think of the relationship. What counts in the end is feeling good. If you win the extra $200 and create an unhappy customer who feels she's been treated unfairly, it's not worth it. If you trade one minute of happiness for a minute of thinking mean, nasty thoughts about someone, you lose. Instead of confronting other people, work with them.

QUICK REFERENCE

What you can do right now:
Whenever you feel that people are about to treat you unjustly, appeal to their own sense of fairness. In the few cases where they proceed to act unfairly, forget about it.

Instead of saying,

"You people replaced my brakes three weeks ago and now they've developed a new squeaking sound. Don't try to tell me that it has nothing to do with your work. I expect you to repair it."

Say,

"You did a nice job replacing my car's brakes three weeks ago. Now I've begun noticing a squeaking sound that wasn't there before I brought it in. What would be the fairest thing to do about it?"

Instead of saying,

"I lost my receipt, but I bought this lawn trimmer from your store less than a month ago. Now it's already broken.

I still have the box it came in, with your store name on it, and I demand that you give me a refund."

Say,

"A month ago I bought this lawn trimmer from your store, and unfortunately it's already broken. I do have the original box with your store name on it and I don't have the receipt. What do you think would be the fairest way to handle this?"

Instead of saying,

"I know my rights, and I demand that you take care of this my way."

Say,

"Considering the facts, what would be the fairest way to handle this?"

38. Let's Look at This Another Way

As Sales Manager, you're given the task of selecting a new office furniture system for your Sales Department. After evaluating several suppliers, you decide that a movable cubicle design is best, and you select one with four-foot-high partition walls. Before signing the purchase order, the Facilities V.P. asks that you review your recommendation with her. She says, "It all looks fine except I disagree with your choice of partitions. Those short ones just don't give enough privacy. We should definitely go with the six-foot-high walls."

Say out loud to yourself:

"Cynthia, I disagree. The six-foot-high partitions cut people off from each other, and that creates a less cohesive feeling in the department. With all that isolation, productivity is bound to fall."

Now say:

"I understand that you favor higher partitions, Cynthia, and I'd like to consider another point of view. True, the taller partitions create a more private atmosphere, and that can be good in many situations. Other Sales Managers have reported that their Supervisors find it more difficult to lead when they're cut off from their employees. In other words, the privacy of higher walls can lead to lower productivity. With our profit goals in mind, we need to consider that factor, too."

Which approach will lead to more cooperative dialogue? Which will result in each party digging in her heels and defending her own choice?

As Co-chair of a major convention's planning committee, one of my jobs was to promote innovative thinking from committee members. One of them, Jason, had a reputation for zany, inspired brainstorms.

This particular convention has always begun with a Friday-afternoon opening "Welcome" speech, followed by a brief cocktail reception and then "Dinner on Your Own." Participants are supposed to have an early dinner, get a good rest, and then wake up alert and ready to roll when the program starts early Saturday morning.

In past years the Friday-night activities have created lots of complaints. The early arrivals at the cocktail party think of the fancy hors d'oeuvres as their dinner. Late arrivals find long lines and empty hors d'oeuvres trays. So good old Jason said,

> *"I know! Since the convention is in L.A., right near the beach, we'll have a beach party. We'll serve hamburgers and beer, play Beach Boys tunes, and everyone will get plenty to eat. It will cost a lot less than those fancy canapés, too."*

The committee agreed that Jason had a wonderful idea, and he immediately went to work making the arrangements. Two months later, the Association's President heard about it. My Co-chair and I both received urgent messages on our answering machines:

> "I totally disagree with this Beach Party thing. It's got to be stopped. I don't want everybody out partying late and then stumbling in, all hung over, for our Saturday-morning sessions."

I felt resistant as soon as I heard the third word of his message. I thought to myself,

> "He appoints a committee, gives us a job, and we do it beautifully. Then he comes along two months later and tells us that what we've done is all wrong. He can plan his own convention!"

My Co-chair, Janet, acted as peacemaker. I don't think she knows the word "disagree." She doesn't use it, and as a result, people listen to her.

> **"George, I understand what he's concerned about, and this is another point of view we need to consider. He has a good point about the drinking and late partying. We don't want people to feel fuzzy when they come in to that kickoff session first thing in the morning. Still, Jason's idea sounds like a lot of fun."**

We realized that the President didn't object to the Beach Party itself; he was concerned about promoting late-night rowdiness. Our real challenge was to find a way to have fun Friday night, let Jason know that we appreciated his creativity, and ensure that everybody would be fresh in the morning.

It didn't take Janet long to come up with the solution: Have the Beach Party, issue each person two drink tickets rather than hosting an open bar, and close it all down at 10:00. That plan would meet every objective.

When she talked with the President, Janet didn't say,

"The Committee disagrees with your idea of canceling the Beach Party."

Instead she began,

"We understand your concern about late-night partying, and we agree that that's not what we want. Instead of just canceling the Beach Party, let's consider some other options."

It looked like we were all going to have a good (but not too good) time . . . until the local chapter's liaison said he **disagreed** with the revised plan.

Nobody wants to be condemned or judged unfavorably; they stiffen, resist, and become combative when told that you "disagree" with them. It's a good term to avoid if you want to promote cooperation with other people.

Tune in "Mr. Rogers' Neighborhood" on PBS, and notice how Fred Rogers promotes nonjudgmental thinking in children. He actively fosters the idea that many people can have different viewpoints and interpret facts uniquely. Taking his "friends" (young viewers) on a museum tour, Fred says,

"And what do you see in that painting? It looks like some kind of chicken to me. You might see a dove, or

some other bird, or something else altogether. Everybody has different ideas."

You'll never hear Mr. Rogers criticize anybody else's idea or put it down. Unfortunately most of us aren't naturally in Mr. Rogers' frame of mind when it comes to negotiating or settling a dispute. It's best to avoid "disagree" and similar terms. Though you may not mean it that way, the other guy is likely to "hear" that you are judging him and labeling his way of thinking as wrong.

Validate others' views and let them exist alongside your own. Instead of saying, "I disagree with you," you'll find people much more cooperative when you say, "I understand your view, and I have another interpretation I'd like to discuss."

QUICK REFERENCE

What you can do right now:
Rather than suggesting that someone else's viewpoint is less valid than your own, accept new ideas and let them coexist alongside yours. Then tap the merits of both approaches and come up with an even stronger alternative.

Instead of saying,

"I disagree with your selection of our official rental car company. Your choice is too expensive."

Say,

"I understand your preferred selection of our official rental car company. Considering our budget constraints, let's talk about some of the other options, too."

Instead of saying,

"I think you're wrong about that paint color. A black bathroom is nauseating."

Say,

"I understand that you like the idea of a really 'different' color scheme for the powder room. Black paint would be one way to do it, and there are some other approaches that could get similar results, too."

Instead of saying,

"I disagree with you."

Say,

"I understand, and I'd like to consider some more viewpoints."

POWER TALKERS . . .

VI. Speak Decisively

When you listen to a Power Talker, you hear someone who gets to the point, does away with unnecessary verbiage, and says exactly what he means. There's so much vague, beat-around-the-bush talk these days that it's a real relief to find someone who chops away wasted wordage and concentrates on communicating concisely and precisely.

Power Talkers are definite about what they say. They make commitments about what they **will** do, not what they'll see if they can perhaps possibly try and maybe do. They're always conscious of projecting an image of reliability.

Communication is a two-way street, and Power Talkers do a good job of listening actively in addition to expressing themselves well. They don't, however, trust that they understand everything just right the first time. They demonstrate their communication skills by taking the time to verify that what they understood is, in fact, what you think you said.

In this section you'll meet people who manifest their reliability with their language. They show their communication skills by confirming their understanding when they're listening, and by using words efficiently and effectively when they're speaking.

39. You Should?—Or You WILL?

While vacationing in the Caribbean, you decide to order a package of fresh tropical fruits and have it sent to your friends back home.

The sales clerk says to you:

"Your gift package should get to Iowa in about a week or so."

Notice the difference if the clerk says:

"Your gift package will arrive in Iowa within five working days."

Which sounds like your friends are definitely going to get their fruit before it rots? Which version leaves you feeling rather indefinite about its arrival?

The salesman returning my phone call said,

"Like I said when I took the order, your screens should be ready in two weeks."

But I had ordered them two and a half weeks ago! The more I deal with people, the more convinced I am that the initial impressions you gain during your very first meeting are pretty darn reliable.

The screen company's fliers had been posted throughout my neighborhood, advertising "Any size screen measured and installed, $14.95." I called for an estimate well before Seattle's brief and wonderful summer began. The answering service operator told me that "Ned should call you back by the end of the day." He didn't. The next day I called again. The operator said, "Well, I don't know what to tell you. He should get back to you right after lunch." I knew he should, but didn't have any faith that he would.

After three days I wrote Ned off as yet another unreliable flake and called a different screen company for an estimate. After I had scheduled my new appointment, Ned finally called! Though I explained that I'd given up on him and called a competitor, he said he'd be in my neighborhood the next day and told me he'd stop by at noon.

He didn't. But he did show up at 4:30 and quickly measured all the windows. Figuring that Ned's prices were about the same as everyone else's, and he had already taken all the measurements, I gave him the order. He said they should be ready in two weeks.

After two and a half weeks without a word, I called and left a message. No callback. Another message. No callback. My third message was, "My screens are late. Return this call today or cancel my order." Ned did call me back, apparently oblivious to his promised (and missed) delivery dates. His old standard "should be ready in two weeks" rang hollow since we'd already passed the two-week point. Time marched on. On the one-month anniversary of our order, I left my final message for Ned:

"Tell Ned he can do whatever he wants with our screens. I'm going to find someone who can keep a promise and place a new order."

Ned called back, promising to arrive by 1:00 the next afternoon. He eventually arrived at 4:45 and discovered that some of the screens didn't fit quite right, altered them with the tools in his truck, and asked for his check as he headed out the door.

I followed Ned out to the driveway and said,

"Ned, I'd like you to know what I think of your service. You took twice as long as you said you would. You ignored most of my repeated messages to call. And you didn't honor one single commitment you made to me. I don't feel that you've treated me well as a customer."

Hardly noticing my obvious frustration, Ned only said,

"Hey, I couldn't help it. With this heat wave, what do you expect? Ninety-nine percent of my customers are happy, and there's always one percent that won't ever be pleased, no matter what. What do you want? I'm not gonna grovel."

I then realized that I had been wrong. Ned hadn't broken any commitments; he had never made any. He never said he **would** do anything, just that he **should**.

QUICK REFERENCE

What you can do right now:
Commit to specific dates, times, and amounts. "Should" avoids commitment and sounds wishy-washy.

Instead of saying,

"That should run about 40 or 50 bucks."

Say,

"Your charge will be $49.95."

Instead of saying,

"You should get this in just a few days."

Say,

"I will mail this first thing in the morning."

Instead of saying,

"We should get this done by . . ."

Say,

"We will get this done by . . ."

40. Give Your Word and Then Beat It!

You work part-time in a local quick-print shop. A customer brings in a large copying job and asks when it will be ready for pickup.

Say out loud to yourself:

"Well, I'll probably be able to have it for you later today. I'll shoot for, oh, probably about 4:00."

Now, say:

"I will have it ready for you today before 5:00."

If you were the customer, which statement would you consider more reliable? Which version is more convincing?

I was surprised when the Room Service waiter said, "We'll have your breakfast delivered to you in 20 minutes." I admit that I felt a little irritable after my delayed flights, late arrival, and short rest the night before.

I awoke at 7:00 A.M. and immediately called in my Room Service order. The 20-minute delivery time I had been quoted allowed me just enough time to shower, get dressed, watch the 7:30 news headlines as I ate, and be down in the seminar room by 8:00 to set up for my 9:00 keynote speech.

By 7:35 I was showered and dressed but still hungry. I called Room Service and asked about my breakfast. "It's on its way, that's all I can tell you." By 7:45 I felt impatient and angry. They had already taken twice as long as they'd promised. My morning routine was thrown off and I didn't like it. Each minute that I waited seemed like ten. Finally, at 7:51, the waiter arrived with my tray. The delay probably wasn't his fault, but I didn't greet him very cheerily. I told him that he was terribly late and grumbled about how much I resent the mandatory tips added to Room Service charges.

Was my 46-minute wait for breakfast unreasonable? Not really, except that I'd been promised delivery in 20 minutes. If the person who took my order had said, "Mr. Walther, I'll make sure you have your breakfast before 8:00," I would have been pleased that it was delivered a few minutes early.

My displeasure stemmed from the gap between my expectations and the hotel staff's performance. The larger that gap—when it's in the negative direction—the greater my dissatisfaction. If they had promised 45 minutes and delivered in 46, I would hardly have noticed. If they had promised a "10-minute express service" and delivered in 46, I would have been even more unhappy than I was. If they promised an hour and delivered in 46 minutes, I'd be pleased.

One of the surest keys to making people happy is to deliver more than you promise. If you call a mail-order company and purchase a sweater, you'll be delighted if it arrives within 10 days—providing they promised delivery within three weeks. If they said you'd have it in a week, you'll be unhappy when it arrives in 10 days. The customers' level of satisfaction is a result of the expectations created by the serving organization.

People count on us to deliver at least what we promise. They react favorably when we beat our promises and unfavorably when we fall short. Most often, we set others' expectations by telling them what we foresee happening. When someone asks you for a commitment, there are three responses you can offer:

1. Don't make a commitment—be vague:

"Well, I'll see what I can do, but I'm not really sure when I'll be able to finish the job. Probably toward the end of the week. We'll just have to wait and see."

Obviously this isn't going to create much support for your image as a reliable professional.

2. Make a hopeful commitment that you may not keep:

"I'll shoot for Wednesday afternoon."

If you finish on Thursday, instead, you've just created dissatisfaction.

3. Make a commitment that you will at least keep, and may well beat:

"I will finish the job before the end of the day, Friday."

Now, when you finish up on Thursday, you're a hero!

Jimmy Calano cofounded the world's fastest-growing, most-successful seminar organization, CareerTrack. I got to know Jimmy early in the company's history when I served as a consultant to their burgeoning telemarketing department. One reason for CareerTrack's enviable success record is the leaders' commitment to delivering more than they promise. When he's planning to send correspondence, Jimmy always makes it a practice to say, "I'll send it tomorrow," even though he intends to send it the same day. That way, if there's an unexpected delay, he'll still be keeping his word. Most of the time, though, he beats it, taking the other person by (pleasant) surprise.

George Patton's formula for success was similar:

"Always do more than is required of you."

The bottom line is this: Whenever you establish expectations for others, be certain that you'll at least live up to them. For best results, exceed them.

QUICK REFERENCE

What you can do right now:
Add a "safety cushion" whenever you make a commitment. Then delight the other person by doing your best to exceed the expectation you've created.

Instead of saying,

"I should be able to finish that report by, oh, let's say the 15th or so."

Say,

"I'll definitely have the report finished before the 17th."

Instead of saying,

"Your order should ship by Wednesday, or maybe Thursday. It kind of depends."

Say,

"Your order will ship before the weekend."

Instead of saying,

"I may be able to get to it by around 2:00 or 3:00."

Say,

"I will get to it before 5:00."

41. I Think I Understand What You Think You Said

You've just taken an order from one of your customers, and it's more complicated than usual. He has requested a special shipping address for this one purchase, and the delivery instructions are complex.

Say out loud to yourself:

"OK, I'm pretty sure I've got that right."

Now, say:

"Let's verify those directions to be sure I understood you clearly."

Which version demonstrates to your customer that you really care about getting things right? Which order is more likely to go astray, get delayed, and ultimately lead to an unhappy buyer?

I really enjoy those General Foods International Coffee flavors that come in little 4.5-ounce cans and cost a lot. "Suisse Mocha" and "Café Français" are my favorites, and at our house, we go through many cans every month. I wish the company would sell the same stuff in larger cans at a lower cost per serving. It bugs me that a substantial portion of the small cans' price goes to pay for the container itself. If they sold the product in five-pound cans at my local warehouse store, I'd happily buy it.

You've probably noticed that many of the foods you purchase today, and many other products, for that matter, have a toll-free telephone number printed somewhere on the packaging. Companies like General Foods rely heavily on customer input so they can make product improvements, clear up confusion, and respond to rumors and crises. If you open a can of food and find flecks of metal inside, the manufacturer wants to know about it immediately. Prominently displaying their 800 numbers is a front-line defensive strategy for organizations that want to hear about—and solve—potentially costly problems before they escalate.

As I waited for the microwave to boil my last cup from yet another Suisse Mocha can, I called the General Foods 800 number to ask if the company had considered selling its coffee in larger containers. A very courteous young man named

Jerry at the General Foods Customer Service Response Center answered and sounded genuinely interested in my views. He stressed that input like mine was exactly what helps the company decide how to change and improve its products.

After explaining why only small cans are used (freshness!), and checking to see if there was anything else I wanted to comment about, he explained that his Marketing Department keeps track of which parts of the country call with what types of questions. He asked for my address and telephone number. After I told him, he said,

> **"Allow me to verify and make sure that I have this correct,"**

and proceeded to repeat exactly what I had just told him.

His simple statement that he would verify my address showed me that he takes pride in performing his work professionally. General Foods must genuinely care about getting things right if they've taken the time to train their reps so carefully.

It's easy to think,

> *"Hey, what's the big deal? So the guy asked to verify an address. Why is that even worth mentioning in this book?"*

The image you personally project to others and to yourself is a composite of many small elements. General Foods' image is built from advertising messages, the colors its designers chose for the coffee can labels, the way the Customer Response Center staff answers your calls, and yes, even the way Jerry verified my address. Each element contributes to the overall impression.

The technique Jerry used to confirm my address information also delivered a message to himself. He said he was verifying ". . . to make sure I have this correct." The message he sent to himself was:

"I'm a professional. I get things right because I take the time and trouble to double-check even something simple like a mailing address."

I also noticed that his phrasing eliminated any possibility of my "hearing" that he questioned my communication abilities. Had I spoken inarticulately and garbled my words while chewing gum, Jerry might have said,

"Gee, it's so hard to understand you. I better verify to make sure you were saying what you meant to say."

He could have asked for verification in a way that I might interpret as an accusation that I wasn't speaking clearly. Jerry, however, took full personal responsibility for getting the address correct.

Professionals like Jerry inspire confidence and respect with everything they do, right down to the way they verify an address. Take the extra step of verifying your communications with others to ensure that you also project that professional, follow-through image. And do it in a way that shows you acknowledge your responsibility for communicating clearly.

QUICK REFERENCE

What you can do right now:
Take an extra moment to verify that you have understood accurately. Do it in a way that shows you accept responsibility for getting the information correct.

Instead of saying,

"You're so hard to understand—I'm not sure I got that right."

Say,

"I want to verify that I understood you clearly."

Instead of saying,

"I think I've got that all straight. If I get lost along the way, I'll give you a call."

Say,

"Let's take a minute to be sure I have those directions all straight. That way I'll be sure to arrive right on time."

Instead of saying,

"I guess that about covers it. I think we understand each other."

Say,

"Let's verify that we're both in complete agreement by wrapping this up with a recap of our understanding."

42. Don't Take "No"—or "Yes"—for an Answer

Your neighbors have invited you over for a barbecue. The day before, you call to see what you may contribute.

Say out loud to yourself:

"Is there anything I can bring?"

Now, say:

"What's the best thing for me to bring?"

Which sounds like you really want to bring something Which question is most likely to trigger the normal—though not necessarily true—response, "Nothing at all, just bring yourselves"?

One of the most challenging tasks any sales trainer faces is disciplining salespeople to stop asking Yes/No questions. Using multiple-choice and open-ended queries helps to uncover buying motivations.

One of my clients sells voice mail services for cellular phone customers. These portable phones are great, providing you're always available to answer calls. Most people who buy and use them do so because "being in touch" is vital in their business lives. While they are driving, mobile .phone users are often talking on the phone, thus blocking incoming calls, unless they have a "call waiting" feature. In other words, people often don't get the constant availability they really want when they invest in a cellular phone.

That's where voice mail comes in. With this service, callers are always greeted in the cellular subscriber's voice. If he's already using the phone or has his phone turned off, the caller hears,

"Sorry, I'm either using my phone or am not available right now. Please leave a message after the tone and I'll get back to you shortly."

This service costs just a few dollars a month and tremendously increases the value of cellular phone service. Still, the Customer Service reps working for my client didn't do all that well selling voice mail service.

What were they doing? Asking Yes/No questions.

"Are you interested in signing up for voice mail service to go with your mobile phone?"

Of course most people said no without even understanding what voice mail is. Once they've heard a prospective customer say no, most salespeople get a little fainthearted, give up, and move on to the next call.

I was hired to train my client's telemarketing staff to do a better job of selling this valuable service. Our starting point was to focus on questions. After a short brainstorming session, we had two dozen good open-ended and multiple-choice questions scrawled out on flip chart pages, such as "How do you use the portable phone in your business" and "When people say they have trouble reaching you on your mobile phone, is it usually because you're away from the phone and don't answer, or because you're already using the phone, so they get a busy signal?"

After shifting away from Yes/No questions to the Open-Ended and Multiple-Choice varieties, sales statistics more than doubled. Many of the reps reported that once they asked the right questions, their customers quickly sold themselves on the benefits of using voice mail.

You ask questions to get information. Yes/No questions give you very little. When you want good information, ask good questions.

When your best friend comes home from the hospital after minor surgery, you really want to know how you can help. If you ask a Yes/No question,

"Is there anything I can do?"

the answer will probably be no. To be a more helpful friend, use a different form of question:

"What's the one thing you'd most like me to do to help you get comfortable?"

Get in the habit of replacing Yes/No questions with multiple-choice and open-ended queries. They produce much more useful information for you to act upon.

QUICK REFERENCE

What you can do right now:
Whenever you ask someone a question, first ask yourself, "Is this a Yes/No question?" If it is, change it to the multiple-choice or open-ended variety.

Instead of saying,

"Is there anything I should get for you when I stop at the store?"

Say,

"What may I pick up for you when I stop at the store?"

Instead of saying,

"I'm considering hiring Mark for a position at my company. Does he have any particular strengths or weaknesses I should know about?"

Say,

"As I consider Mark for a position at my company, which of his personal strengths and weaknesses should I keep in mind?"

Instead of saying,

"Are there some features you really want in a new computer?"

Say,

"What are the features you really want in a new computer?"

Instead of saying,

"Do you have any questions?"

Say,

"What questions do you have?"

43. Say It!

You're being interviewed for a new job and the Personnel Director asks about your accomplishments at your previous employer.

Say out loud to yourself:

"Well, that's a really good question and I'm glad you asked it. First of all, one thing I'd like to say is that, generally speaking, my department was sort of a mess before I took over. Within six months, more or less, it ran fairly smoothly."

Now, say:

"My proudest accomplishment was reorganizing the department I led. It was very disorganized when I was promoted to the Manager position. Over the first six months we implemented a five-phase action plan that cut unnecessary paperwork by 30%."

Which sounds like the person you'd consider more seriously for any position? Who seems to be beating around the bush?

I sat in on one client's meeting with his attorney and was amazed at how little was said, and how many words it took to say it. The client wanted to know if it was legally permissible to tape record phone conversations between employees and customers. This is a complicated issue, as state and federal regulations may both come into play. Still, the answer should have come pretty close to "Yes" or "No."

Instead, the lawyer rambled on:

"Well, that's a very interesting issue you've raised, and I'd like to give you my views on it. Understand, of course, that these are just my opinions at this point in time. I would tend to think that—and keep in mind, of course, that this area is subject to a number of interpretations—it would be quite common to assume that certain legal considerations do color, or slant, an employer's ability to do so. Now, let me ask you something. What I would like to know is . . ."

I tuned out and so did the client. Why couldn't the lawyer just say, "Yes, if you have a beep tone on the line." Or, "No, not under any circumstances." Or even, "Yes and no: For calls to customers who are out of state, the more liberal federal regulations do permit taping; for intrastate calls, you may not record conversations under any circumstances."

I guess if you're paid by the hour—and thus by the word—it's advantageous to beat around the bush for a while. All those lawyer jokes must have sprung from clients' firsthand experiences. They're not all loquacious, of course. My own lawyer gets high marks for giving clear, concise answers. (Thank you, Scott!)

I'm not out to pick on lawyers; a lot of people talk a lot without saying much. I'll list some of my favorite pet peeves here, and you'll probably think of a dozen other examples to add.

At this point in time. Doesn't that mean "now"? I have a business associate who invariably uses this phrase. The only justification I can come up with is that he may think it sounds a little more fancy than "now." But it doesn't. It makes him sound self-important. For the phrase "at this point in time," substitute "then." Whenever you can say something in fewer, simpler words, do.

Can I ask you a question? You just did! Why make one question into two? When the time is right, go ahead and ask. You don't need to ask permission to ask a question.

Can I interrupt you? A poll of Americans' biggest communication beefs published in *USA Today* ranked unnecessary interruptions right at the top. The best strategy is always to hear the other person out and then respond. If someone is wandering away from the point, it's better to politely interject your comment without first asking permission.

I would tend to think that . . . Sounds wishy-washy. Say what you believe without first setting up a qualifying safety cushion to cover yourself in case your opinion proves unpopular or wrong.

I was going to say . . . This phrase adds nothing and may well undermine the impact of what the person proceeds to say. It's rather like "It was just a thought, and it may not be worth bringing up, but I guess I will anyway, so here's what I was going to say."

Kind of, sorta . . . There's a whole category of vague qualifiers that diminish the impact of what people have to say. These indefinite qualifiers add nothing to your meaning: dump them!

May I ask who's calling? Flying to a speaking engagement in Canada, I sat beside Gene Monroe, Vice Chairman of Huntsville, Alabama's, largest business-equipment dealer. He saw me working on the manuscript for this book and asked what it was about. As soon as I told him, he said,

"What I really hate is having someone ask if it's OK to ask who I am. I always say no. That really throws 'em. Why do they ask the question if they aren't prepared to deal with the answer?"

Call screeners seem to give little thought to their questions about a caller's identity. If you're greeted with, "May I tell him who's calling?" and the secretary later returns to the line and advises you that he's in a meeting, don't you immediately suspect that you've been deemed Not Important Enough to be put through? A much more effective and courteous way to ask is to explain the benefit to the caller: "Please give me your name so I can prepare him for your call or schedule a callback."

I would say . . . Are you going to? Why not just say it? Is there an "if" upon which the statement is contingent? What does the conditional "would" contribute, anyway?

Can you spell your name? One of my favorites! I'm always tempted to answer, "Yes. In fact I learned how several years ago, and I've gotten quite good at it." What you really want to know is how the name is spelled, so I recommend asking your real question in a courteous fashion: "Please spell your name for me."

There's a great need for straight-shooting, get-to-the-point talk in business. Think of the phone charges, paper, postage, and computer time that we could save if people just said what they meant. And the meetings! I'm an advocate of standup meetings. I've heard waste-conscious managers say that all chairs should be removed before beginning routine staff meetings. It's just too easy to get settled in for a long session half-listening to people verbally wander. You can sit in a chair fairly comfortably for 60 to 90 minutes; you can stand on your feet for about half as long. People get to the point faster when they're on their feet.

Speaking economically and decisively doesn't just save time; it can also inspire confidence in your listener. When you use lots of unnecessary words, it can seem like you're trying to hide something, or like you're really not sure of what you're saying.

Customer Associates at Pacific Bell are trained to

reinforce customers' purchase decisions with decisive, benefit-oriented statements. Rather than saying,

> "I think it'll probably work out pretty well for you. Hopefully, that service should give you just about what you're after,"

trainers stress the importance of making unequivocal statements:

> **"This is going to be just right for you. I know you'll find the service to be exactly what you need."**

The word, "hopefully," all by itself, undermines any chance of being heard as a decisive speaker.

> "Hopefully this will change things,"

doesn't offer much hope. It's much stronger to say,

> **"This will improve your situation."**

A Power Talker is not cold, unfriendly, stingy with words, or mechanical in his communication style. He's someone who does away with unnecessary verbiage, makes his point, and moves on. There's a big difference between patiently comforting a friend who is in trouble and raising a question or making a point in business. A Power Talker is flexible and uses the communication style that's appropriate to the situation.

QUICK REFERENCE

What you can do right now:
Know what you want to say and say it!
    Instead of saying,

> "One thing I'd like to say is . . ."

    Say it!

Instead of saying,

"Do you mind if I ask you a question?"

Ask it!
Instead of saying,

"Well, generally speaking, one thing I would sort of tend to think is . . ."

Say,

"I believe . . ."

POWER TALKERS . . .

VII. Tell the Truth

Power Talkers prize integrity. People who are dishonest may feel that they get more rewards out of life than those who are always truthful. They may cheat to buy happiness. Though tangible wealth may contribute to happiness, material things are not the signs of true success. Many of the world's financially super-rich people are emotionally destitute. In the end, the good guys do win. Do you know any dishonest people who are truly happy?

Power Talkers let you know that they are 100 percent honest by eliminating integrity-busting phrases such as "To tell you the truth." When someone says, "Well, to be absolutely honest with you . . . ," don't you think to yourself, "Does that mean that he's usually not honest?"

In the chapters ahead, you'll be reminded of the powerful benefits of being consistently honest. You'll also see how difficult it is to conceal a streak of dishonesty. As a Power Talker, you constantly affirm your integrity with your choice of expressions and manner of speaking.

44. To Be Honest with You

You've just met an investment advisor who wants to win your trust and your business. You ask him about the performance of his own investment portfolio, and he responds,

"Well, I have to tell you the truth, to be perfectly honest . . ."

Which way do you run?

In my first conversation with Mr. M., a promoter who booked me for a series of public seminars in Poughkeepsie, he said,

"We're working on booking the new Bardavon Opera House for your program. I have to tell you the truth, we could sell out all 1000 seats for each of the three seminars."

I'm immediately wary when someone makes a point of prefacing supposedly truthful statements with phrases like, "I have to tell you the truth . . ." If a person is habitually honest, if his integrity is 100%, why would he need to make a point of explaining that he's about to tell the truth?

A month before the scheduled program date, he called me to explain that ticket sales were miserable:

"Well, to be completely honest with you, our marketing information in the computer was slightly off and we may have to start from scratch. Could we possibly push the date back a couple of weeks?"

One peculiarity I noticed about this promoter was that he had no home phone number. In case of a last-minute flight interruption en route to an engagement, I want to be able to reach the meeting planner. Mr. M. said his home was his refuge; the phone rang enough during work hours. Later I learned that he didn't have a house. He lived in his parents' basement and used their phone! So much for this big-time promoter.

Each time I asked for a firm count of the audience size, his answer was evasive:

"Well, frankly speaking, anything could happen. There may be a last-minute surge of sales. Don't worry, we'll invite students at a local school to fill up all available seats."

Finally, the big day arrived! Julie and I flew to New York and were picked up at our Manhattan hotel in a somewhat shabby rented stretch limo. Mr. M. apologized,

"I'm sorry we had to pick you up with the car. Unfortunately, to tell you the truth, the corporate helicopter is taking one of our clients on a sightseeing trip today."

(Later it became clear that he and his company didn't even own a beat-up Ford Pinto, let alone a helicopter.)

"Well," I said, "the seminars begin first thing tomorrow morning. How many tickets did you end up selling?"

"Well, ah, to be completely candid, ah, I don't know the final figure, but ah, to tell you the truth, it looks like there may be only a couple of hundred."

"For each of the three seminars?"

"No, for all three seminars combined."

"Don't tell me that you've booked me into a 1000-seat opera house and we'll have less than a hundred people in each audience! It's going to look and feel like the program is a flop."

"Oh no, don't worry, we've moved the location to a nearby hotel's meeting room that'll be just the right size."

The next morning I walked into the meeting room, ready to set up my props and adjust the projector. There were only

25 seats. That turned out to be OK. Mr. M. had sold only 18 tickets!

Part of my agreement with the promoter was that the balance of my speaking fee would be paid before the program began. Standing outside the seminar room, he began patting his pockets when I asked for my check.

"Oh gee, to tell you the truth, I think I may have forgotten my checkbook."

My conversations with Mr. M. became interesting performances in themselves. I started to enjoy asking him for a simple, honest answer and then listening to him squirm and wriggle with some phrase that belied his innate dishonesty.

I did begin presenting the first of my three seminars without the promised payment, and explained that I would not begin the second one until he had visited the bank and secured a cashier's check.

I was surprised when, as I ended the first seminar three hours later, he returned with the strangest-looking check I've ever seen. Although it bore none of the customary pre-printed account information, it did have three different signatures scrawled on it, as well as a neatly affixed "certification label" in the upper left corner. It looked like a case of overkill, as if Mr. M. had said to some bank clerk friend:

"Look, to be perfectly honest, this speaker wants a certified check, but, well, to tell you the truth, I just won't have the funds until the end of the day. Could you maybe take one of those blank counter checks and stamp it a few times, and scribble some signatures on it, and stick some kind of label on it so it looks really official?"

The next morning, after completing the three seminars with a grand total of fewer than 100 in the combined audiences (just slightly shy of Mr. M.'s "honest" assurance of 3000), I went to three different branches of the bank on which the suspicious check had been drawn. Officers at each one looked at it skeptically and said they'd never seen a check quite like it. None would cash it.

It's sad, and true. Completely honest people are rare. Think of all the people you've known. There are a few who always do exactly what they promise, always tell the truth, and are completely trustworthy. And there are many whose honesty is well below 100%.

Even people who have a high sense of personal ethics use integrity-busting phrases. It's a habit that's easy to change—and well worth changing.

Be committed to complete honesty in your behavior and show it with your language. The rewards from establishing a reputation for 100% integrity last throughout your lifetime. Not only will others be much more willing to work with and trust you, you'll also enjoy the feeling of self-respect that results from knowing you are a person of unwavering character.

QUICK REFERENCE

What you can do right now:
When everything you say is totally honest, there's no need to alert anyone that you're about to tell the truth. Eliminate "integrity-busting" expressions that suggest you aren't always sincere and forthright.

Instead of saying,

"To be perfectly honest . . . ,"

BE perfectly honest.
Instead of saying,

"Well, to tell you the truth . . . ,"

ALWAYS tell the truth.

45. Just Say No!

A colleague at work asks you to pitch in and help him with a project. You're feeling pressured about your own workload and have no time to spare. Still, you don't want to disappoint your co-worker.

Say out loud to yourself:

"I'm awfully busy with my own work, John, but, well, I guess I could try to help you. I don't know if I can get to it, but I'll try and see what I can do."

Now, say:

"John, I'm completely committed to my own projects and cannot help with your assignment now. I suggest that you ask Tony. He's familiar with your department."

Which version are you likely to regret later on? Which is the more truthful approach?

My professional speaker colleagues don't generally like clients to videotape their presentations. When they do permit it, they normally charge a substantial fee. Speakers want to avoid the all-too-common nightmare of a client taping their presentations with poor-quality home video equipment, catching them on an off day, and then distributing the unedited tapes. Thousands may view them and conclude that a speaker isn't very good, based on that one bad tape.

In May 1990 I left my wife and our newborn daughter behind and flew to Detroit for a freebie. A member of my staff (since terminated!) had agreed to waive my fee for a seminar promoter, even though his was not a nonprofit organization—the only situation in which I'll give a free speech.

But I believe in keeping my word, and even though the

client wasn't a nonprofit organization, he had been promised a free speech by my assistant, and I honored my employee's commitment. I didn't relish this engagement from the start, and I had made a commitment.

In the final week before the presentation, the promoter had called and offhandedly mentioned that he videotapes all programs for promotional use. Rather than asking for my permission, he used a ploy commonly attributed to slick, manipulative salesmen. "You don't have any problem with that, do you?" Instead of telling him how I really felt, I said it'd be OK. He agreed that I would be given the only master cassette of the tape and that brief clips from his copy would be used only for promotional purposes.

Immediately after hanging up, my inner voice said,

"Wait a minute, why are you agreeing to this? You don't want to go do this free speech in the first place; something smells fishy about the whole thing."

Upon my arrival at Detroit's Sheraton Southfield hotel, I found just what I had begun to suspect: a very low-budget operation. The promoter was arranging chairs, setting up tables, and attending to logistical details himself. At this point, though, I couldn't turn back. Once I'm on-site, my responsibility is to the audience. I knew that 650 people were looking forward to that evening's event.

An hour before starting time, a young man named Charlie walked in with his VHS camcorder. He was the promoter's longtime friend and had offered to tape all of the seminars in exchange for free tickets.

As it was, the program did go very well. The audience was attentive and responsive, the "video crew" unobtrusive, and I felt good about my performance. At the conclusion I received an enthusiastic ovation, autographed many books, and saw hundreds of happy audience members head for home, eager to put the seminar ideas into practice.

As the hotel staff began folding up the chairs and tables, I asked Charlie for my video master. He looked surprised and said it belonged to him, but offered to make me a copy. I firmly told him that the master copy was mine, and explained my agreement with the promoter. He said, "No, I keep the master. It's mine, but you may have a copy if you'd like."

Charlie was not a timid young man, and insisted quite firmly that the original master tape was his. I insisted that it wasn't.

Then Charlie came up with his hypocrisy jab:

"I've just been listening to your seminar, getting great ideas, and admiring you as a superb communicator. At this point, though, I feel that the way you're communicating with me is totally out of sync with what you've been saying during the speech."

And Charlie was absolutely right. After several minutes of our tense exchange, he "got me" with the truth. My communication behavior had been inconsistent with what I'd been saying on the platform. As a result, we were having a very uncomfortable exchange. Although we hadn't actually shouted, I had asked him to hand me the master so that I could stomp on it, thus ending the discussion about who would "own" it.

Our exchange turned the corner only after I responded to his hypocrisy charge:

"Charlie, you're right. I haven't communicated well with you. I haven't really been honest. Here's the truth: I feel taken advantage of. I didn't want you to tape me in the first place. I was advised just a few days ago that you would be here, and I should have insisted on adhering to my normal agreement that permits taping only with professional equipment, for payment of an additional fee. I haven't felt right about any aspect of

your taping and should have denied permission right from the start."

Charlie's face relaxed and he smiled. "Now I understand," he said. "You should have told me that right from the start."

We finally agreed that he'd forward the original master to me after dubbing a copy for promotional use only. We called the seminar promoter over and reviewed our agreement together. And we ended up with a friendly understanding.

The lesson was an obvious one. When you don't want to say yes, don't. I had, and the result was a tense, charged atmosphere and temporary ill-will. Had I stuck to my convictions from the start, I could have avoided the entire confrontation.

When you halfheartedly agree to do something that you really don't want to do, you almost always regret it later. If you aren't sure you really want to do it, it's best to just say no.

While preparing the manuscript for this book, one of my neighbors called and asked me to help her with a "little project." She wanted help writing a letter to the real estate developer who's expanding our community. I'm concerned about the development issues she raised, and have already made many contributions to our neighborhood group. I was tempted to just go ahead and write the letter for her. By the time I'd have met with her, reviewed the draft, and so on, the "little project" would have taken away at least two hours from my much more important book-writing priority. So I said:

"Sandy, my attention is fully dedicated to writing my new book right now. I know you'll do a fine job writing the letter on your own. No, I won't help you write it."

I felt so good about saying no! I didn't intend to be rude or uncooperative; I was simply drawing the line.

We all take on tasks and chores that we don't really want to do. The result is usually that we do them halfheartedly, feel bad about it, and regret that we said yes in the first place. It's much better to say no when that's what you really feel.

QUICK REFERENCE

What you can do right now:
Before you agree to do anything you're only half-sure you want to do, take a time-out. Decide if you'll be able to do a great job, enjoy doing it, and finish it without interrupting your other more important priorities. If you decide that you don't really want to do it, say no.

Instead of saying,

"Well, I really don't have the time to help you, but I'll see if maybe I can squeeze in an hour or two for you."

Say,

"No, I'm sorry. You'll be better off getting help from someone who can really get involved."

Instead of saying,

"Gosh, it's an honor, and I don't know quite what to say. I'm not sure, but I guess I'll be able to serve on the PTA Board."

Say,

"Thank you for honoring me with your invitation. I'll carefully assess my workload and other commitments and give you an answer by the end of the day."

Instead of saying,

"I don't really want to, but I guess I'll say yes."

Say,

"No, I won't. I do appreciate your asking."

46. Never Say Always

You've just purchased more plants for your living room after seeing yet another African violet wither away, just as the Boston fern did two weeks ago, and the philodendron before that.

Say out loud to yourself:

"Everything I try to grow always dies. I can't ever get any plant to stay alive for more than a month."

Now, say:

"Some of the plants I've been growing stay fairly healthy for a while, and then I'm not sure what happens. I'm going to find a houseplant book and figure out what I should be doing differently."

Which version sounds like you should just give up and buy silk flowers? Which shows you're going to improve on your track record?

I could see her paper plate tipping 10 degrees, then 15 degrees, then 20 degrees. The wedding was at a yacht club, which didn't explain her listing dish; we were ashore in the club's banquet hall. The sixtyish woman in front of me in the reception buffet line was attractive and vivacious. Her plate was heaped with shrimp, roast beef, macaroni salad, and, for some reason, a little pile of salted peanuts. She was waiting for—and concentrating on—the champagne-pouring bartender as her plate angled precariously. At 25 degrees, the first peanuts started to roll toward me, and I could visualize the whole melange slopping off the plate and onto my shoes.

"Excuse me, your food's just about to spill."
"Oh, don't mind me. I'm always spilling everything. Hah,

I'm such a jerk! I'll spill anything. I'm probably going to spill this champagne, too! I always do."

Her self-denigration, though delivered jokingly, left me thinking that her self-esteem must be in pretty rough shape. She probably says that she always messes everything up— whether she's talking about cooking, playing the stock market, or anything else. Even though she seemed jolly, I felt sorry for this woman. She didn't think much of herself.

You know how uncomfortable it is to be around a couple that's having marital trouble. They have a couple of drinks, then start pouring out their mutual disgust.

"If she hadn't made us so late, I'd have helped with the barbecuing. She just never can get ready on time. She's always late."

"Me? He's the one who misplaced the car keys. He's always losing them. In fact he always loses everything. On our first date he even lost the concert tickets."

You want to stop them, but it's too late. They've already plunged into inaccurate universals: always, never, everything, nothing.

Universal statements are rarely true and they're hardly ever constructive. Is it possible that he **always** loses the keys, and **everything** else? Does the woman in line at the wedding reception **always** spill **everything**?

The most important place to start when eliminating universal terms from your vocabulary is with yourself.

"I can't believe I did it again! Every time I print something out on the computer, I always forget to switch from the dot matrix printer back to the laser printer. I never do get that right. What's the matter with me?"

This kind of self-abuse can't help change the situation. It's much more productive to replace the universals with more accurate modifiers:

"Sometimes I forget to change the printer switch. I'm getting better about remembering, and I don't always get it right. Now I'm going to concentrate on setting the printer switch correctly."

Whether commenting on your own behavior or someone else's, eliminate untrue universal terms and replace them with accurate descriptions of what's really happening. You'll be doing yourself justice and encouraging others to cooperate with you, too.

QUICK REFERENCE

What you can do right now:
Be alert for and eliminate universal terms like "always," "never," "everything," and "nothing," especially when using them to criticize someone else's performance or your own.

Instead of saying,

"I can never remember your phone number."

Say,

"Sometimes I have trouble remembering your number, so I'm going to write it down in my day planner book."

Instead of saying,

"You always pull in too far when you put the van in the garage. Can't you ever get it right?"

Say,

"When you leave me plenty of room in front of the van, it's much easier for me to get at my workbench. I appreciate it."

Instead of saying to yourself,

"Everything goes wrong every time I try to negotiate with him. I always end up on the short end and I never get treated fairly."

Say,

"Sometimes my negotiating techniques haven't brought about a positive outcome. Next time I'm going to use another approach."

VIII. Get Back to Basics

I've been fascinated by Robert Fulgham's phenomenal success with his best-seller, *Everything I Need to Know I Learned in Kindergarten*. It's so true. Winston Churchill was right when he said, "All the great things are simple. . ."

Having come this far in *Power Talking*, you've probably said to yourself many times, "These techniques are so simple!" And indeed they are. Power Talkers aren't particularly skilled at making things complicated; they don't employ any high-falutin' tricks. They are careful to speak positively, express appreciation, be optimistic, accept responsibility, be cooperative, say exactly what they mean, and tell the truth.

That's about all there is to it, except for three more basics: *Get people's names right, say "Please" and "Thank You," and when you're wrong, say you're sorry.*

This last section doesn't need any introduction. If you were spotty in your application of the preceding 46 techniques, and just made sure you remembered to always practice these last three without fail, you'd be way ahead of most folks. Power Talkers remember the basics.

217

47. The Name Game

Waiting to be seated at a restaurant, you vaguely recognize a diner who gets up from his meal and approaches you. His name doesn't come to mind.

Say out loud to yourself:

"I'm terribly sorry. I know I should remember your name, but I just can't think of it."

Now, say:

"It's nice to see you, I'm . . ."

Which is the more socially confident version? Which statement sounds more self-assured and which sounds weak?

I was shopping at one of those office supply warehouse stores, sampling the various felt pens, when a familiar woman approached and said, "Hi, there! I thought I recognized you."

I used to feel awkward when I didn't remember someone's name. I'd launch into the old standby "don't-hurt-their-feelings" excuses you hear all the time. Realistically, though, even a memory expert doesn't remember everybody's name. You and I definitely don't. When you've forgotten someone's name, do away with unnecessary verbiage, avoid belittling yourself, and always tell the truth.

I realized that I wouldn't remember this woman's name. As I opened my mouth, prepared to say,

"Please remind me of your name,"

she cut me off, saying,

"George, I'm Sandy Wilson, from PNSA. It's nice to see you."

Of course! I know Sandy and have talked with her on the phone and at meetings several times. She didn't leave me in the awkward position of having to explain that I'd forgotten who she was.

We skipped over the common social exchange about forgetting names and renewed our acquaintance quickly. I respected Sandy for taking the initiative.

When you deal with people, names are important. Fortunately, when you attend a convention, delegates usually wear badges proclaiming their names. You can discreetly glance down (as they do, too) and refresh your memory, maybe even appearing to have remembered on your own. But out in real life, you often have to ask.

One key to developing rapport with other people lies in knowing and using their names. Dale Carnegie reminded us long ago that the sound of a person's own name is the sweetest sound to anyone, in any language. We've all learned that developing a talent for remembering and using names can be a tremendous asset in business. You can easily excel in each of the three most common situations that come up when dealing with names: When you've forgotten theirs, when they've forgotten yours, and when you've first met (and not yet forgotten.)

1. Don't Lose Face Over a Forgotten Name.

The best way to handle forgetting a name is very simple. Accept it! You've forgotten a name—so what? Why worry about it? The other guy may have forgotten yours, too, and certainly has forgotten plenty of others'.

The next time you attend a party, bump into a long-forgotten colleague or customer at the airport, or end up in the Safeway line behind a new neighbor you've recently met, say,

"Please remind me of your name."

That's all. It's direct, courteous, and positive. It avoids that usual cumbersome, tucked-tail explanation: "Oh, I'm terribly sorry, but I just can't seem to remember your name, although it's right on the tip of my tongue." Leave out the embarrassment. There's no ignominy or disgrace about it. You've forgotten the name. You want to be reminded. Period.

2. And If You Suspect They've Forgotten Yours . . .

Self-assured, confident, powerful people announce their names when they see you. Even when chances are that you probably do remember theirs, they make it easy on you. They begin a conversation by reaching out for your hand, and as they shake it, say, "I'm Heather White. We met at the Nashville convention last year. It's nice to see you again."

Your best bet when seeing someone who may have forgotten your name is to say,

"Hi, I'm _____, nice to see you."

There's a built-in bonus to this approach: They'll probably respond with their own name, so if you've forgotten it you're already covered.

3. When You Hear It, Use It.

Most people don't really **forget** a name they used to remember, they just fail to remember it in the first place. Since names are vital in developing rapport and strengthening relationships, it's worth taking some simple steps toward improving your name memorizing techniques. The easiest thing to do is use a name right away once you've heard it.

A not-very-successful salesman once said to me:

"Yes, George, I've been very successful in sales. And you know, George, it's really not too hard to do very, very well once you've mastered the basics. One of the things I always try to do is use the other person's name during the conversation. And as you well know, George, that's especially important on the phone. It really grabs the other person's attention. But, George, you just can't please everyone. In fact, just the other day I talked to a guy from Iowa who, well, what he said, George, is, 'You seem slick when you use my name too much,' No Kidding, George . . ."

Yikes! Screeching fingernails on a blackboard, I found myself counting how many times he said my name, wanting to interrupt and say, "You idiot! Why didn't you listen to that Iowan?"

Here's a simple guideline: *Use the other person's name three times in a conversation.* First, right after he says it. Second, sometime during the conversation, and third, as you end it.

Taking a couple of simple steps to ensure that you remember and use someone's name makes them feel good, and helps you feel good, too.

Your business life and personal life are both built around interpersonal relationships. Knowing and using people's names counts for a lot. Get in the habit of remembering and using them right from the start.

QUICK REFERENCE

What you can do right now:
Consciously use people's names three times during conversations. When you meet someone for the first time, immediately use his name and remember it. And when you see someone who may have forgotten your name, remind him right away. If you've forgotten his, ask him to remind you.

Instead of saying,

"I'm sorry, it's right on the tip of my tongue, but I just can't seem to think of your name."

Say instead,

"Please remind me of your name."

Instead of saying,

"You probably don't remember my name, but . . ."

Say instead,

"Nice to see you again, my name's _____ ."

Instead of saying,

"Gee, I'm sorry, but I just can't remember your name."

Say instead,

"Hello again. I'm _____ . Please remind me of your name."

48. What's the Magic Word?

It's Friday afternoon and your secretary has once again worked through lunch to be sure that your handouts are ready for the presentation first thing Monday morning.

Say out loud to yourself:

"I don't know how I'd get by without Christine. I wish the rest of the clerical staff were half as conscientious about deadlines as she is."

Now, say:

"Christine, I really appreciate you. Thank you for doing such excellent work on the handouts, and for giving up your lunch hour. I'm very grateful for your dedication, and I enjoy working with you."

Which version will ensure that Christine "keeps up the good work"?

A retired neighbor of mine devotes much of her time to fund-raising for the American Cancer Society. She works tirelessly and has achieved great results that benefit many seriously ill patients.

Recently, she called my wife in desperation.

"Julie, I'm in a terrible fix. Our biggest fund-raising event of the year is right around the corner and we don't have the tickets promised in our promotional literature for the auction. Do you know anybody who could make a big donation? One or two airline tickets would be ideal."

My mother died of cancer, so I definitely have a personal interest in wanting to help beat this disease. One of our best friends, Kevyn Leincr, was at that time a Sales Manager for USAir. He's a great friend and a generous person, so he was our "target." Everything was right down to the wire, so the neighbor gave us a letter explaining the auction, and we faxed it to USAir immediately. Within 48 hours Kevyn came through with two unrestricted free tickets anywhere in the USAir route system, worth up to $3000. No strings.

When the auction took place, Julie and I were in England on a speaking tour. We returned home, expecting to find a Thank-you note and copy of the American Cancer Society's formal letter to USAir and Kevyn. We found nothing.

Although we saw the neighbor from time to time, we never really stopped to talk with her. I felt somewhat resentful that she hadn't thanked Julie, who was responsible for initiating the airline contact in the first place, and whose friendly persuasion convinced Kevyn to deliver.

Months later, I said to Kevyn,

"You know, that woman from the American Cancer Society never even had the courtesy to thank Julie for contacting you about the ticket you donated."

Kevyn's response:

"Oh, they never thanked me, either. It happens all the time. You'd be surprised how many charitable organizations ask for contributions, neglect to say please, and then never follow up in any way."

The point of the story is this: It's foolish, stupid, and ungracious to overlook simple courtesies like saying please and expressing appreciation. After all the neighbor's hard work, the lasting impression with us, and with USAir's Sales Manager, is negative. I presume the ticket fetched a good price, and that the ACS benefited. The neighbor, though, will find a cool reception if she turns to USAir or to us next year.

She didn't mean to be rude, I'm sure. She just overlooked one of the basics. She allowed her hard work to be overshadowed by a careless slip.

It's so easy, and so rare, to be genuinely courteous toward people who mean a lot to us—especially customers. And the payoff is phenomenal. One standard rule of thumb among sales professionals is that it costs at least five times as much to win an order from a new customer as it costs to win one from an existing customer. In my work as an advisor to Fortune 1000 companies, I've never found the figure to be that low. Organizations that have bothered to take a close look find it's at least ten times as costly to win new customers' business.

When I serve as a consultant to marketing organizations, I often begin by asking,

"What are you doing to let your existing customers know that you appreciate them?"

The answer is nearly always revealing and embarrassing.

Sales forces typically invest huge amounts of time, money, and personal energy chasing after new customers. And then they drop the ball.

One of my most popular speaking topics deals with reducing customer "churn." I use a visual analogy of a conveyor belt. Picture a long conveyor belt about 3 feet wide, moving away from you at a steady clip. You're standing at one end of the belt, alongside a salesperson, and the belt moves away from you, off into the distance. In my speeches, I show three slides depicting that conveyor belt.

The first shows the eager, enthusiastic salesperson lavishing attention on a new customer—let's call him Harry— helping him step up onto the belt. This corresponds to the most common, and most expensive, task in any marketing organization: *Winning new customers.* Using a combination of advertising, trade show exhibits, direct mail campaigns, telemarketing calls, and often, face-to-face sales appointments, we set out to convince prospects to buy something from us, to "get them on the conveyor belt."

My second slide shows the same conveyor belt scene. Now the salesperson is attentively schmoozing another prospect, hoping to convert him into a customer. Harry has now progressed in his relationship—moved along on the conveyor belt. He may even have made a couple of repeat purchases. The salesperson, though, is concentrating his attention on the new prospect, seeking to get him on the belt and convert him into a customer. Meanwhile, our friend Harry is glancing at his watch, thinking,

"It's been a while since I got much attention from my salesperson. I was very important to him just before my first purchase and now I'm feeling taken for granted."

The salesperson, of course, is hardly aware of Harry's feelings of being neglected. He's too busy winning new customers to pay much attention to the second big task in marketing: *Keeping customers on the conveyor belt.*

In the third slide, we see the same salesperson again. Sure enough, he's attentively convincing yet another new prospect to become a customer, to get on the conveyor belt. We see other customers who've recently begun their relationship with the company moving along into the distance, just as Harry did. And there's Harry, far down the belt, jumping off. He's on his way to jump onto some competitor's conveyor belt. They've begun making him feel important and appreciated again.

Most salespeople completely neglect the third task in marketing: *Find out why customers are getting off your conveyor belt.*

An organization's "churn rate" refers to the rate at which new customers become disenchanted and fall off the conveyor belt. In every business, a customer relationship may be thought of as a stream of expected future cash flow. That's especially evident for firms in the membership and subscription businesses. It costs them (and every other type of business) a lot to win a new customer. Take cable TV, for example. If a customer signs up for cable service and then cancels just a few months later, the company will lose money on the account. To stay in business, it has to actively seek new customers to ensure an adequate future cash flow to cover its fixed expenses. When one of these customers cancels his cable service, and the company has to replace him, it's dealing with churn.

A high churn rate is extremely costly. Think of what happens when you cancel your cable TV service. Several clerks are involved in closing your account and generating the paperwork to wrap things up. A service representative is dispatched to your home or apartment building to sever the cable connection. The computers are reprogrammed to delete your account number. But those are just the obvious costs.

We've got to consider the cost of winning another new customer—of getting him on the conveyor belt—to replace the missing cash flow represented by the unhappy customer who has just jumped off. For a cable TV company, that means more advertising, direct mail, telemarketing, special incentives, and even door-to-door sales calls.

Why does churn happen? One of the most oft-repeated statistics on the seminar circuits of the late 1980s came from the Wisconsin Restaurant Association. That study revealed that when a restaurant's patrons stop eating there and are asked why, they cite the following reasons:

1% Died
3% Moved away
5% Developed other relationships
9% Preferred a competitor
14% Were dissatisfied about the product (meal)
68% Felt an attitude of neglect or indifference

I know of no wide-reaching national research to determine why customers fall off conveyor belts, but those percentages look pretty accurate to me. I've had several clients conduct expensive studies to get their own answers. Top place always goes to the same reason: Customers feel taken for granted.

Once marketing executives grasp the true costs of customer churn, they want to know the most effective way to reduce it—to keep customers on the conveyor belt longer. The easiest way is ridiculously simple: Remember to say please and thank you.

It's so easy—and profitable—to improve the customer retention efforts in any business. You don't need to send expensive gifts or conceive a complicated customer appreciation campaign. A simple, sincere, personal thank you is all it takes.

Personal relationships can be a lot like customer relationships. Friendships and marriages can wither from the same tendency to neglect common courtesies. You can easily apply the same "conveyor belt principle" to your nonbusiness relationships. Your success at building and maintaining any kind of relationship depends on the same three skills: Initiating, Nurturing, and Recapturing. Whether it's your marriage, a close personal friendship, or a casual relationship with a neighbor, think in terms of getting 'em on the conveyor belt, keeping 'em on, and finding out what's wrong when they fall off.

Power Talkers remember the basics. They never fail to say please and thank you when it's the gracious thing to do. And they don't wait until it's expected. Every now and then they send a postcard, call a customer back, or drop in to thank a helpful neighbor. Parents who teach their children that "please" and "thank you" are magic words aren't exaggerating.

QUICK REFERENCE

What you can do right now:
Remember to exercise common courtesies in relationships with others, particularly those you may take for granted. Don't be stingy with "please" and "thank you."

Instead of saying,

"Those people at the dry cleaners sure do a nice job."

Say,

"Thank you for always treating me so well and taking good care of my clothes. I appreciate your excellent service."

Instead of saying,

"We've got to find a way to get 1000 new customers this quarter."

Say,

"I'm going to make absolutely sure our present customers know how much we appreciate them."

Instead of saying,

"My wife? Yeah, she's great. She feeds the baby, cooks good meals, keeps a lovely home and works hard. I'm lucky."

Say,

"Darling, I appreciate you. This weekend I'm going to do something special to let you know how much I mean it when I say, 'Thank you.'"

Instead of saying,

"They know I appreciate them."

Say,

"Thank you."

49. Say You're Sorry

Following an audit of your expense account, the Branch Manager calls you to her office and asks about a meal receipt that doesn't appear to have been business-related. Sure enough, it turns out that you charged a family dinner to your company credit card three months ago.

Say out loud to yourself:

"With all the paperwork we have to do around here, I'm surprised there was only one incorrect charge. I'll bet everybody here has a few personal meals slip through now and then. You can't blame me for making a mistake once in a while."

Now, say:

"You're absolutely right, that was a personal meal and it should not have been charged to my expense account. I'm sorry I didn't catch it myself and I will be extra careful in the future. It's my mistake and I apologize."

Which sounds like the most trustworthy employee? Whose reaction do you respect? Who will the Branch Manager be more likely to recommend for promotion?

When you phone an airline to make a reservation, a pizza chain to place your order, or your bank's Customer Service center to inquire about a recent account statement, your call is handled by an Automatic Call Distributor, or ACD, before you talk with an agent. Today, this type of electronic device is used in almost every large telephone center.

One major advantage of an ACD is that it helps callers connect with exactly the right person. The ACD analyzes each incoming call and quickly identifies which 800 number the caller dialed, what part of the country he's calling from, and in some cases, the specific telephone he's using. Then it directs his call to an agent who specializes in the questions he's most likely to ask. Telephone center managers rely on ACDs because they provide very helpful statistical analyses of representatives' performances. For every employee, supervisory group, work shift, or hour of the day, the manager knows how many calls were made or answered, how long the average call lasted, how much time the rep spent processing paperwork, and so on.

Managers pay careful attention to a key ratio called the "percent time available/unavailable." When an individual rep is clipping along, handling lots of calls with only a very brief pause between each one, his "availability" to talk with customers is high. When a rep is procrastinating, taking unnecessary time with his paperwork, chatting with co-workers, and avoiding customer contact, his ratio shows a high "unavailable" percentage.

One of my client's call center managers decided to post a report of all reps' individual statistics on the bulletin board. To avoid peer embarrassment, she substituted employee I.D. numbers for names. Two reps, Stanley and Stephanie, both checked the report and noticed that their ratios were unfavorable. They were handling fewer calls (and taking longer to do it) than their co-workers.

As a consultant to many call center managers, I have yet to discover a completely foolproof system for measuring performance (or allocating commissions, or fairly scheduling work shifts, or anything else). There's always someone who will outsmart whatever system management implements.

Stanley outsmarted the ACD in his call center. He figured out that the device counts how many minutes his phone is busy, how many calls he handles, and how long his conversations last. It doesn't "listen in" to see whom he's talking with or even if he's talking at all.

So Stanley began calling his home phone and letting it ring for three minutes, then hanging up and calling again, and then hanging up and calling again. The ACD counted each as a customer call. The next time statistics were posted in the lunch room, Stanley's numbers showed dramatic improvement! The average number of calls handled each day soared from 47 to 92! According to the statistics, he was on the phone almost all the time. His average call length was right in step with the average for other reps. He appeared to be very productive.

Stephanie, a new employee, had been struggling to improve her performance statistics. Good ol' Stanley showed her how to do it. Overnight, her stats also showed amazing improvement.

Of course the manager noticed these dramatic changes and asked both employees what was going on.

Stephanie admitted her tricks, accepted personal responsibility for what she had done, apologized, and stopped doing it. Her performance continues to legitimately improve and her future with her employer is bright.

Stanley blamed his performance on the pressured environment. That ended his employment.

When I was in college at the University of California, Santa Barbara, I landed a dream job. I was hired to be the TWA Campus Sales Representative. The money wasn't much; the benefits, though, were incredible! As a 20-year-old student with an unlimited air travel pass, I asked myself each week:

"Shall I stay around campus this weekend, drop a couple of dollars at the theater, spend a few bucks on meals, and shoot a few games of Eight-Ball? Or shall I catch the polar flight to London, see two movies going over and two more coming back, enjoy four nice inflight meals, sightsee for a few hours in England, and spend zero dollars?"

I didn't spend many weekends on campus.

As an airline sales representative, you inevitably deal with some of your customers just after they've returned from a horror flight on your airline. I remember being verbally assaulted by the Men's Choir Director after he'd taken his boys on a European tour. I escorted them as far as Frankfurt, then bade the group farewell as they continued on to sing for some Austrian Countess and harmonize in several European capitals. I headed off to visit a friend in Berlin before returning home.

Two weeks later, back on campus, I was blasted by the Director:

> *"I'll never fly on TWA again! Your airline lost our entire group's luggage on the flight from Rome to Paris. You canceled our flight from Madrid to L. A. and instead sent us home via Lisbon, Philadelphia, and Kansas City. What have you got to say?"*

My boss and mentor at TWA, Paul Oglesby, was a hulking giant who'd been a lineman for the Raiders before injuries forced him out of professional football. One of the most important lessons he taught me was:

> **"When you're wrong, make no excuses. Say sincerely, 'You are absolutely right and I don't blame you for feeling upset. I'm sorry we screwed things up for you.' "**

After the Choir Director's tirade crescendoed, I followed Paul's advice and sincerely apologized without making excuses. Next year the Men's Choir again flew TWA on its European tour.

When the Chrysler Corporation was accused of resetting new car odometers back to zero after executives had driven them for personal use, what did Lee Iacocca do? He admitted the truth, made no excuses (in fact, he said Chrysler had been "dumb" to do it), apologized personally on the company's behalf, and offered settlements to the affected owners whose "new" cars really hadn't been unused. Dishonesty cost the company at least $26 million in penalties and settlements. Criminal fines alone could have exceeded $100 million if the Chairman had not chosen to be forthright. But he told the truth. As a result, the company's performance remained strong in the face of the potentially devastating publicity. The Chairman himself bolstered his respected image as an honest straight-shooter.

Follow Paul Oglesby's advice: When you are personally wrong, or when the organization you represent has mistreated a customer, it's always best to admit the mistake, accept responsibility, apologize, promise to do everything you can to correct it, and immediately begin following through.

QUICK REFERENCE

What you can do right now:
Whenever you make a mistake, admit it readily and say you're sorry. Defuse potential emotional flareups, avoid confrontations, and build others' respect for your character by facing facts, admitting the truth, and apologizing.

Instead of saying to yourself,

"With all these people drinking red wine, he'll never figure out that I'm the one who stained his new sofa. He probably won't even notice it until the morning."

Say,

"Wayne, I'm sorry, but I spilled wine on your sofa. Let's get some stain remover or soda water on it right away before it sets overnight."

Instead of saying,

"Don't blame me if the client files are out of order. Other people use them, too, you know."

Say,

"I'm sorry you had trouble locating the right client files. I'll go through and check them all before Friday."

Instead of saying,

"Look, it's just too bad. Don't blame me. I couldn't help it."

Say,

"I'm sorry; it was my responsibility."

IX. Share Their Pride

A true Power Talker is not content to bolster his own image and self-esteem, he makes sure that he's enriching others, too.

I began writing this book with an underlying mission. My drive welled up from a need I have experienced personally. Reflecting back, I now realize that many of my choices in life have been motivated by one common desire: to be acknowledged and applauded. I've found that I'm not alone.

This last chapter is my most important message to you.

50. The Sound of One Man Clapping

You've just read the draft of a long-term strategic plan for your organization prepared by an interdepartment project team you put together. It's outstanding.

237

Say out loud to yourself:

"Boss, this is the strategic plan my project team has developed. They did some fine work; it's the best plan we've had around here in a long time. They should be feeling pretty pleased with themselves."

Now, say:

"Team, I'm proud of every one of you who worked on this project. You've done an excellent job, and I'm going to make sure that the boss knows exactly how proud of you I am. After I've reviewed it with her, I'll give you point-by-point feed-back. For now I want you to know your excellent and hard work is very evident. Thank you."

Which sounds like the leader whose team members will feel that their work was truly appreciated? Who's making a big mistake by assuming that his team feels appreciated?

My dad, Merle Walther, was born in 1908 and grew up in Sacramento, California. His large family—five children, of which my dad was the youngest—didn't have much money. Dad did have a penchant and talent for playing sandlot baseball. He was well known in the local leagues and was apparently a terrific first baseman. So good in fact that a scout from Detroit recruited him to play professional ball. Dad thinks of the afternoon when that scout came to his house as a near-religious experience. His dream was to play in the big leagues, and he imagined how proud his family would be as he became a famous baseball star.

Sitting in the humble front room my grandfather, John, had built in a converted barn, the scout asked for permission to take Merle back to Detroit so he could join the team. Dad recalls what his father said:

*"I've heard about those baseball players. They drink.
They smoke. They chase women. And after a few years,
their careers are over. I won't hear of it. My son's going to
go to college."*

Dad was heartbroken, but there was no arguing. After all,
Grandpa John was a German "head of the household," and
when he said NO, that was that. I'm sure Dad resented his
father's decree all his life. He yearned to play baseball.

Sure enough, Dad went off to college and did quite well
studying electronics. He got a good job with the Pacific Telephone and Telegraph Company and specialized in microwave transmissions.

When World War II broke out, he volunteered to join the
Navy and became a radar officer on a destroyer escort in
the South Pacific. I'm sure he played a lot of baseball on the
Navy teams when they were ashore.

And then, after the war, I was born. What do you suppose
Dad wanted me to do? Right. Play baseball.

As a kid, I remember Dad playing catch intensely with me
in the front yard. For me it wasn't fun, it was torture. But
Dad wanted to work me hard so I'd be the baseball star his
father hadn't let him become. He forced me to sign up for
Little League.

I showed an early inclination toward sales. Neighbors and
family friends all said I had the gift of gab. I always sold the
most Scout-O-Rama tickets and founded a succession of
neighborhood sales enterprises peddling greeting cards, firewood, extension cords, trivets, used comic books, and Sno-
Kones. I could succeed selling anything. Baseball just
interfered with my sales activities.

I don't recall Dad ever congratulating me for being such a
whiz-bang little salesman. He often pointed out that his son
was a disappointing ball player.

Finally I summoned the courage to tell Dad that I would
not join Little League the following season. So he joined, as

the Chief Umpire. Poor Dad. He must have felt terribly ashamed when the other umps asked why his son didn't play on one of the teams.

Through my high school years, Dad continued to volunteer as a Little League umpire. I continued to avoid team sports. I was now active in the Junior Achievement program, winning sales contests and being chosen by my high school peers to head our model companies. Dad didn't acknowledge my business acumen, he just wished I would play baseball.

At high school graduation, I received many top academic and service honors, but none for athletics. Dad pointed that out, too.

In university, I majored in Rhetoric and Public Address, and graduated *summa cum laude*. Dad didn't say he was proud, only that he wished I had at least tried out for the college baseball team.

In graduate school I'd call Dad to tell him how well I was doing with my MBA program classes and he'd try to tell me how well the San Francisco Giants were doing. Finally he'd give up, saying, "Of course you don't give a damn about baseball. You never have. You're a zero in sports."

Years later, when I completed my first book, *Phone Power*, it struck me that of all the subjects I could have written a book about, I chose telephones. Dad had by now retired from a 40-year career with a telephone company. It seemed I was doing everything I could to win his approval. Except play baseball.

When the publisher sent me my first copy of the completed book, fresh from the printer, I inscribed it to Dad and sent it to him.

"Dad, you may never realize how much of my business success has been the result of striving to make you proud of me."

As I complete this book that you're reading, Dad still hasn't read *Phone Power*, and he hasn't once commented on my inscription.

A few years ago I presented a speech in San Francisco and invited Dad to be my guest in the audience. He'd had many opportunities before, but hadn't shown up. Even now, as a retired, lonely man (my mother had died some years earlier), he said that he probably wouldn't make it to my speech. Although he was in superb health, and the hotel ballroom was less than half an hour from his home, he complained that:

"Parking's impossible in San Francisco. And I'm sure as hell not going to pay some damned valet car parker fella three or four bucks just to park my car."

Well, Dad did show up. And I was in top form. As I ended my presentation, Dad stood up and began to applaud, biting his lower lip. I've enjoyed many wonderful ovations, but none was ever as loud as the sound of that one man clapping.

My eyes moisten, right now as I type, as I remember how I felt when Dad said the words I'd yearned to hear all my life:

"Son, I'm proud of you."

Whenever I share that story with my audiences, several people come up to the stage at the end of the program. Their eyes are red and they say,

"My mother/father was just like that. She/he never did say 'I'm proud of you,' though I wanted very much to hear it. What is it about your parents that makes it so hard for them to say it?"

Once I've opened up, others do. And it turns out that we're all pretty much alike. As I'm telling the story of my dad and his wish that I'd be something I'm not, I see many in the audience reacting emotionally. Instead of approaching me after the applause, I hope they proceed directly to the pay phones in the lobby and call the people they're proud of.

It's remarkable how common this striving for appreciation is. In Kirk Douglas's autobiography, *Ragman's Son*, he traces most of his life's achievements back to his struggle to be noticed and appreciated by his father. He never got the satisfaction of hearing his dad say that he was.

After 10 years as cohost of ABC's "Good Morning America," Joan Lunden recalled her life and career for an article in *Parade* magazine. Her father died piloting his small plane when Joan was 13.

> *"Up until then, I'd had a pretty comfortable life. But then all of a sudden the bottom dropped out, and my security was gone. I think that's when I first decided that I would always rely on my own strength and be in control of my own life."*

The interviewer concluded by asking if, with a strong marriage, unpretentious life, three beautiful daughters, and a $10 million contract, she is content.

She paused and looked at her husband playing in the yard with one of their little girls and said,

> *"My biggest regret in life is that my father didn't live to see my success. If he's up there watching, I'm sure he's extremely proud of what I'm doing. And I don't just mean my job. I mean that I have a lovely family, that I live right and have the kind of values he would have wanted me to have."*

After a decade of strained relations, my dad and I got together at last. The speech in San Francisco, when he finally said "I'm proud of you," was a milestone in our relationship. When I explained how much I wanted him to be proud of me, his response was,

"You must be kidding. Since the day you were born, I've been telling every friend I have how proud I am of you. Don't you know that?"

Well, now I know. And it feels great.

I've always thought my career choice is quite revealing. I stand onstage before hundreds or thousands of people, working hard to earn their appreciation. For years, their ovations helped compensate for my dad's failure to tell me that he was proud of me.

As William James said,

"The deepest principle in human nature is the craving to be appreciated."

You can be sure that most of the people you'll ever meet are striving to be noticed and applauded. It's a natural instinct, and one that goes unfulfilled in many. The people you know and work with are hungry for appreciation. They're probably not getting enough of it from the people they love.

If you do nothing else after reading this book, please call the people you love and tell them why you're proud of them. Do it now.

QUICK REFERENCE

What you can do right now:
Let the people you feel proud of hear about it.

Instead of saying,

"That daughter of mine is a wonderful student. Everyone likes her. And she's so beautiful. I'm proud of her."

Say,

"Sweetheart, I'm very proud of you. You're a wonderful student, you choose great friends, and you're gorgeous."

Instead of saying,

"That Gordon has a great future here. He's doing fine work in my department, and I suspect he'll be headed for the Home Office in a year or two. He should feel very proud of himself."

Say,

"Gordon, you are handling your career beautifully, and your work is very valuable to the company. I know you have an excellent future here. I'm proud of you."

Instead of saying,

"Our organization does a great job of putting on superb workshops that help a lot of people."

Say,

"Barbara, since you've been the Executive Director of our association, we've never had a finer management team. I want you to know that I'm proud to be a member of our association."

Instead of saying,

"I'm sure he knows I'm proud of him."

Say,

"I'm proud of you."

POWER TALKERS . . .

X. Do It Now

Power Talking positively affects all areas of your life—**once you start using it.**

There are three critical steps in becoming a Power Talker: (1) Decide you're going to change, (2) Build a support system to keep you on course, and (3) Track your own progress to keep up the momentum.

1. Decide to Be a Power Talker.

Choose to project a more positive image for yourself, enhance others' cooperation with you, accelerate your career progress, and enjoy more positive, fulfilling relationships.

As you read the examples in this book, you notice that they're down-to-earth. You don't need to be some corporate big shot to benefit from using Power Talking in your life. These principles work whether you are a salesperson, a supervisor, someone who's just starting your career, or an established leader of your organization—and they're just as beneficial to parents, friends, consumers, and anyone else.

Are the Power Talking techniques difficult to master? Certainly not. There are no new words to learn and there's nothing tricky about applying the principles.

Once you make the decision, the action is easy.

2. Build a Support System.

Teaming up with a partner is the single most important action you can take toward becoming a Power Talker. Invite someone you work with, live with, or enjoy a strong friendship with to become a Power Talker, too. There's nothing like a companion who's tuned in and listening for power*less* phrases that may slip out during your conversations. Agree to help each other by remaining vigilant about each other's language. You could use a subtle reminder like winking or clearing your throat, or you could be a lot more conspicuous. Some Power Talkers write the powerless phrases they're purging on wide rubber bands and wear them around their wrist. When their partners hear them slip, SNAP!

For maximum results, form two or more partnerships covering your professional and personal lives. If you have children at home, help prepare them for the real world by sharing the Power Talking principles. It takes very little incentive to enlist their zealous support in cleansing your vocabulary. Offer a kid a quarter every time he catches you saying "but" instead of "and," and you'll soon break old habits.

Supportive "Power Talking" Quick Reference Cards and audio/video programs are also available to help reinforce these concepts. For ordering information, see page 267.

3. Keep Track of Your Progress.

You will notice the difference Power Talking makes in your own daily life, and you'll also become very aware of powerless talkers around you. Each time you hear someone say, "I'll be honest with you," or "I just got lucky," or "I'd hate to," or "I'll try," you'll notice the negative impression that phrase makes on anyone listening. And that will serve as a reminder to keep up your own steady progress.

All 50 Power Talking phrases are summarized in the "Quick Reference" section that follows. As you master each one, note your successes and reward yourself. Remember, though, that Power Talking isn't a final destination at which you arrive. It's a continuing journey, so enjoy your trip.

I've enjoyed my journey while writing this book for you, and have benefited tremendously from the process of listening for examples and translating them into principles. Thank you for reading.

More Power Talking to You!

George R. Walther

Quick Reference Summary

Use the following pages as a quick reference summary to remind you of the 50 Power Talking techniques.

Power Talkers . . .

I. PROJECT POSITIVE EXPECTATIONS

1. *I'll be Glad to!*

Each time you begin to say "I'll **have to**," substitute a phrase that shows you'll be **glad to**. Notice the difference it makes in your own mood and in others' attitudes about co-operating with you.

Instead of saying,

"I'll have to do it."

Say,

"I'll be glad to do it."

2. *Will You Try, or Will You DO It?*

Tell yourself and everyone else what you **will** do, not what you'll **try** to do.

Instead of saying,

"I'll try to do it."

Say,

"I will do it."

3. Say What You Want to Do
Use "I want to" to describe the positive outcomes you envision rather than saying what you'd "hate to" have happen.
Instead of saying,

"I'd hate to give you the wrong information."

Say,

"I want to help you get the right information."

4. I Haven't Yet and I CAN
When describing your capabilities to yourself or to someone else, eliminate "I can't" from your vocabulary.
Instead of saying,

"I can't do that."

Say,

"I haven't yet done it and I can."

5. Refuse to Be Helpless
If you feel sick, supplement prudent medical attention with personal action. Use your language to promote a positive attitude and strengthen your body's natural disease-fighting powers.
Instead of saying,

"My condition is hopeless; I can't change it."

Say,

"I can improve the quality of my life."

6. Better When Than If
When you hear yourself starting to ask a conditional "If . . ." question, rephrase it to incorporate your positive expectation.

Instead of saying,

"I was wondering if you can . . .?"

Say,

"When will you . . .?"

7. It's No Problem!
Substitute "challenge" or "opportunity" for "problem" and concentrate on exploring solutions.

Instead of saying,

"I'm afraid that's going to be a problem."

Say,

"That sounds like a challenging opportunity."

8. Self-Fulfilling Prophecies Come True
Replace habitual self-limiting phrases with empowering assertions.

Instead of saying,

"I'm no good at that."

Say,

"I'm getting better at that."

9. Get a Return on Your Investments
Substitute "invest" for "spend" when you talk about how you'll use your time, money, and other resources.

Instead of saying,

"I'm going to spend some time and money taking night classes."

Say,

"I'm going to invest some time and money taking night classes so I'm ready to move ahead in my career."

10. Nothing's Impossible

Banish the word "impossible" from your vocabulary. Substitute a more accurate and positive phrase to describe what appears infeasible.

Instead of saying,

"This is impossible."

Say,

"This is going to require some special effort, and it can be done."

11. Kids Are All Ears

Be especially conscious of Power Talking whenever you are around youngsters. Set an example and help shape kids' futures by speaking positively to and about them.

Instead of saying,

"You're a bad child and you're always getting into trouble."

Say,

"You're a good child, and that behavior is not acceptable."

Power Talkers . . .
II. GIVE CREDIT WHERE DUE
12. What's Your Excuse?

Stop making excuses and apologizing for some imagined shortcoming. Either change it or forget it.

Instead of saying,

"You'll have to excuse my car/mess/hair/house."

Say,

Nothing!

13. It's Just My Opinion

You're not "just" or "only" anything. Describe yourself, your beliefs, and your accomplishments positively and proudly.

Instead of saying,

"I'm only just the . . ."

Say,

"I am the . . ."

14. Is "Luck" Getting the Credit for Your Hard Work?

When you succeed, modestly acknowledge your own role in attaining your accomplishments, both to yourself and to others.

Instead of saying,

"I got lucky."

Say,

"I planned well and worked hard."

15. What They Don't Know Won't Hurt Them

You're probably far more critical of yourself than anybody else will be. Go ahead and enjoy doing as well as you can.

Instead of saying,

"I'm really not too good at this."

Proceed to do your best without excuses.

16. Ken and Spencer Were Right!

Go out of your way to compliment people and give them credit for doing things right, especially when they don't expect it.

Instead of saying,

"That daughter of mine is a big help around the house."

Say,

"Darling, you are a big help around the house, and I appreciate it."

17. You're About as Old as You Say You Are

Use neutral or positive phrases in reference to advancing age. Don't erode vitality by speaking negatively about aging.

Instead of saying,

"I feel worse and worse. I'm getting too old."

Say,

"I feel good."

Power Talkers . . .
III. REBOUND RESILIENTLY

18. Does Your History Repeat Itself?

When you're confronted with a "failure," look for the lessons you can learn and grow from the experience.

Instead of saying,

"I failed."

Say,

"Here's what I learned . . ."

19. Half Empty or Half Full?

Rephrase negative reactions to unexpected changes and

say, "This is great news. It means that . . . ," and then start looking for the positive result that can follow.

Instead of saying,

"I see some very negative consequences resulting from this turn of events."

Say,

"I see some very positive consequences resulting from this turn of events."

20. If Only I Had . . .

Focus your attention—and your language—on what you will do to positively shape your future. Don't dwell on the unalterable past by talking about what might have been.

Instead of saying,

"If only I had."

Say,

"Starting now, I will."

21. Bottoming Out

When you're at a low point, write out your affirmations, using positive language, and say them aloud to yourself. Don't just think, act.

Instead of thinking to yourself,

"I'm a loser."

Say,

"I am a winner."

22. Bouncing Back

When you hear yourself describing a setback situation as

a terminal disaster, rephrase your description to recognize that you will bounce back and move ahead.

Instead of saying,

"I'm going under."

Say,

"I'm going to bounce back."

23. It's Over!

When things seem to be headed for a disastrous outcome, stop and ask yourself, "What's the very worst thing that could happen?" Accept that eventuality as if it were true and say, "That's all; it's over." Then, get to work applying your energy to create a more positive outcome.

Instead of saying,

"This is terrible, and it could get a lot worse."

Say,

"Even if the worst happened, I could live with it. So there's no point worrying. That's all; it's over. Now I'm going to work on making things better."

Power Talkers . . .
IV. ACCEPT RESPONSIBILITY
24. Watch Where You Point That Thing!

Be on the alert for that pointing finger! Whenever you hear (or see) yourself directing blame or responsibility elsewhere, focus on the three fingers that point back at you.

Instead of saying,

"You make me upset when . . ."

Say,

"I feel upset when . . ."

25. Use the Time You Have

Purge phrases that suggest time is out of your control—that there's not enough of it. Acknowledge your personal responsibility with your language.

Instead of saying,

"I just can't get caught up; I don't have enough time."

Say,

"I can get caught up by managing my time and eliminating low-priority projects."

26. It's Not What Happens to You, It's What You Do About It

Accept personal responsibility for your present situation and decide to move forward rather than wasting energy by blaming your current condition on past circumstances.

Instead of saying,

"I can't help it; it's someone else's fault."

Say,

"It's my responsibility to change things."

27. You Can Count on Me

Even though you may not be the person who'll actually perform the tasks, accept personal accountability when you offer to help someone.

Instead of saying,

"That's not my area. You'll have to get someone else to help you."

Say,

"I'll help you by getting your message through to the right department."

28. *Do You Choose to Lose?*

Avoid "victim" language; acknowledge your responsibility by using the word "choose." When you're unsatisfied with the way things are, choose to change them.

Instead of saying,

"I can't change things, I didn't get myself into this fix."

Say,

"I choose to make the best of this situation."

Power Talkers . . .

V. ENCOURAGE COOPERATION AND REDUCE CONFLICT

29. *Get That "But" Out of Your Mouth!*

Make a conscious decision to replace "but" with "and" as you talk to yourself and to others. Notice that your thinking "opens up" as ideas coexist instead of conflict.

Instead of saying,

"I can see that it's a good product, but it's expensive."

Say instead,

"I can see that it's a good product, and it's expensive."

30. *Let's Do It!*

Whenever you seek others' input and suggestions, stimulate a free flow of ideas, no matter how crazy some might seem.

Instead of saying,

"That's not practical, it'll never work."

Say,

"That's an unusual approach, let's go with it and see where we end up."

31. Do ME a Favor for a Change

When you need someone's cooperation, figure out why his participation will benefit him, not you. Emphasize the benefits he'll realize by following your suggestion.

Instead of saying,

"Will you do me a favor?"

Say,

"Here's why this will be good for you."

32. You Get What You Ask For

Make it a habit to ask at least one relationship-improving question every single day.

Instead of saying,

"Is everything satisfactory?"

Say,

"How can I do a better job for you?"

33. So, What CAN You Do?

Whenever you start telling someone what you can't do, change your focus and substitute a statement indicating what you can do.

Instead of saying,

"Here's what I can't do."

Say,

"Here's what I can do."

34. Breaking the Language Barrier

When you're involved in a conflict, use your language to show that you're intent on working **with**, not **against** the other person; show that you're on the same side of the table, working as a teammate.

Instead of saying,

"I understand what you want. But I must adhere to my policies."

Say,

"We share some important common goals. Let's see how we can work together."

35. You're Invited!

When you want others to cooperate with you, "invite" them to do so, and give them a choice about what they'll do.

Instead of saying,

"Here's what you'll have to do."

Say,

"I invite you to choose the approach that will work best for you."

36. I Recommend

Whenever you set out to "sell" an idea, service, or product, focus on the benefits to the other person and use the word "recommend" to close the sale.

Instead of saying,

"One thing you might possibly want to consider is to . . ."

Say,

"I recommend that you . . ."

37. What Sounds Fair to You?

Whenever you feel that people are about to treat you unjustly, appeal to their own sense of fairness. In the few cases where they proceed to act unfairly, forget about it.

Instead of saying,

"I know my rights, and I demand that you take care of this my way."

Say,

"Considering the facts, what would be the fairest way to handle this?"

38. *Let's Look at This Another Way*
Rather than suggesting that someone else's viewpoint is less valid than your own, accept new ideas and let them coexist alongside yours. Then tap the merits of both approaches and come up with an even stronger alternative.

Instead of saying,

"I disagree with you."

Say,

"I understand, and I'd like to consider some more viewpoints."

Power Talkers . . .
VI. SPEAK DECISIVELY
39. *You Should?—Or You WILL?*
Commit to specific dates, times, and amounts. "Should" avoids commitment and sounds wishy-washy.

Instead of saying,

"We should get this done by . . ."

Say,

"We will get this done by . . ."

40. *Give Your Word and Then Beat It!*
Add a "safety cushion" whenever you make a commitment. Then delight the other person by doing your best to exceed the expectation you've created.

Instead of saying,

"I may be able to get to it by around 2:00 or 3:00."

Say,

"I will get to it before 5:00."

41. *I Think I Understand What You Think You Said*
Take an extra moment to verify that you have understood accurately. Do it in a way that shows you accept responsibility for getting the information correct.

Instead of saying,

"I guess that about covers it. I think we understand each other."

Say,

"Let's verify that we're both in complete agreement by wrapping this up with a recap of our understanding."

42. *Don't Take "No"—or "Yes"—for an Answer*
Whenever you ask someone a question, first ask yourself, "Is this a Yes/No question?" If it is, change it to the multiple-choice or open-ended variety.

Instead of saying,

"Do you have any questions?"

Say,

"What questions do you have?"

43. *Say It!*
Know what you want to say and say it!
Instead of saying,

"Well, generally speaking, one thing I would sort of tend to think is . . ."

Say

"I believe . . ."

Power Talkers . . .
VII. TELL THE TRUTH
44. To Be Honest with You
When everything you say **is** totally honest, there's no need to alert anyone that you're about to tell the truth. Eliminate "integrity-busting" expressions that suggest you aren't always sincere and forthright.

Instead of saying,

"Well, to tell you the truth, . . ."

ALWAYS tell the truth.

45. Just Say No!
Before you agree to do anything you're only half sure you want to do, take a time-out. Decide if you'll be able to do a great job, enjoy doing it, and finish it without interrupting your other more important priorities. If you decide that you don't really want to do it, say no.

Instead of saying,

"I don't really want to, but I guess I'll say yes."

Say,

"No, I won't. I do appreciate your asking."

46. Never Say Always
Be alert for and eliminate universal terms like "always," "never," "everything," and "nothing," especially when using them to criticize someone else's performance or your own.

Instead of saying to yourself,

"**Everything** goes wrong **every time** I try to negotiate with him. **I always** end up on the short end and I **never** get treated fairly."

Say,

"**Sometimes my negotiating techniques haven't brought about a positive outcome. Next time I'm going to use another approach.**"

Power Talkers . . .
VIII. GET BACK TO BASICS
47. The Name Game
Consciously use people's names three times during conversations. When you meet for the first time, immediately use his name and remember it. And when you see someone who may have forgotten your name, remind him right away. If you've forgotten his, ask him to remind you.

Instead of saying,

"Gee, I'm sorry, but I just can't remember your name."

Say instead,

"**Hello again. I'm _____ . Please remind me of your name.**"

48. What's the Magic Word?
Remember to exercise common courtesies in relationships with others, particularly those you may take for granted. Don't be stingy with "please" and "thank you."

Instead of saying,

"They know I appreciate them."

Say,

"**Thank you.**"

49. Say You're Sorry

Whenever you make a mistake, admit it readily and say you're sorry. Defuse potential emotional flareups, avoid confrontations, and build others' respect for your character by facing facts, admitting the truth, and apologizing.

Instead of saying,

"Look, it's just too bad. Don't blame me. I couldn't help it."

Say,

"I'm sorry; it was my responsibility."

Power Talkers . . .
IX. SHARE THEIR PRIDE
50. The Sound of One Man Clapping

Let the people you feel proud of hear about it.
Instead of saying,

"I'm sure he knows I'm proud of him."

Say,

"I'm proud of you."

An Invitation from the Author

To arrange customized Power Talking or Phone Power presentations for your organization, I invite you to call my office 24 hours a day: 1-206-255-2900. I'm proud to personally present programs for leading corporations and associations worldwide. I am honored to hold the National Speakers Association's highest award for speaking skills and professionalism, the CPAE.

Many highly effective Power Tools are available to help you implement Power Talking throughout your organization and in your own personal life. They include audio and video cassette programs suitable for corporate training and individual use, plus easy-to-use quick reference cards and progress-tracking systems.

For a Fax Brochure describing Power Talking and Phone Power support materials, please fax your request to: 1-206-235-6360 and include a return fax number and address.

I'm now gathering ideas for *50* **More** *Power Talking Techniques* and look forward to hearing your examples. I'll be pleased to credit you when they're used in the next edition.

George R. Walther
6947 Coal Creek Parkway, Suite 100
Renton, WA 98059
1-206-255-2900   Fax: 1-206-235-6360

Suggested Reading List

Blanchard, Kenneth and Norman Vincent Peale. *The Power of Ethical Management*. New York: Ballantine Books, 1989.

Blanchard, Kenneth and Spencer Johnson. *The One Minute Manager*. New York: Berkley, 1987.

Calano, Jimmy and Jeff Salzman. *CareerTracking*. New York: Simon & Schuster, 1988.

Carnegie, Dale. *How to Stop Worrying and Start Living*. New York: Simon & Schuster, 1984.

Davis, Wynn. *The Best of Success: A Treasury of Success Ideas*. Lombard: Great Quotations, Inc., 1988.

Douglas, Kirk. *The Ragman's Son*. New York: Simon & Schuster, 1988.

Dyer, Wayne W. *What Do You Really Want for your Children?* New York: Avon, 1985.

Fulghum, Robert. *All I Really Need to Know I Learned in Kindergarten*. New York: Villard, 1989.

Hill, Napoleon. *Think & Grow Rich Action Pack*. New York: E. P. Dutton, 1988.

Mackay, Harvey. *Beware the Naked Man Who Offers You His Shirt*. New York: William Morrow, 1990.

——————. *Swim With the Sharks Without Being Eaten Alive*. New York: William Morrow, 1988.

Mandino, Og. *The Greatest Salesman in the World*. New York: Bantam Books, 1988.

Martorano, Joseph T., and John P. Kildahl. *Beyond Negative Thinking*. New York: Plenum Press, 1989.

Murphy, Joseph. *The Power of Your Subconscious Mind*. New York: Bantam Books, 1982.

Peale, Norman Vincent. *Positive Imaging*. New York: Ballantine Books, 1982.

——————. *The Power of Positive Thinking*. New York: Ballantine Books, 1990.

——————. *Why Some Positive Thinkers Get Powerful Results*. New York: Ballantine Books, 1988.

Schwartz, David Joseph, Ph.D. *The Magic of Thinking Big*. No. Hollywood: Wilshire Book Company, 1959.

Seligman, Martin. *Learned Optimism*. New York: Random House, 1990.

Seligson, Tom. "I Decided to Always Rely on My Own Strength" (Profile of Joan Lunden), *Parade* magazine, September 9, 1990.

Ziglar, Zig. *Raising Positive Kids in a Negative World*. New York: Ballantine Books, 1989.

About the Author

George Walther is in great demand as a consultant and speaker for leading corporations and associations worldwide. He shows business and professional leaders how to communicate more positively on the phone and in person.

He is the author of *Phone Power*, first published in the U.S. by G. P. Putnam's Sons in 1986 and now available in paperback, as well as foreign language, audio, and video editions.

George earned a B.A. in Rhetoric and Public Address, and an M.B.A. in Marketing from UCLA's Graduate School of Management.

He is one of fewer than 100 people worldwide to have been honored with the National Speakers Association's highest award for speaking skills and professionalism, the CPAE. He regularly addresses audiences around the world.

Corporate clients include Ford, Du Pont, Hewlett-Packard, GE, and numerous other Fortune 1000 companies. A wide range of associations including ASAE, Sales and Marketing Executives International, and the American Management Association also hire him to speak at their conventions.

George lives with his wife, Julie, near Seattle. Their first child, Kelcie Paige, was born while George completed the *Power Talking* manuscript. When not onstage delivering a speech, George can be found with his wife and daughter enjoying long walks in the woods.

▨▨▨ BOOKS FOR SUCCESS ▨▨▨

__THE ULTIMATE SECRET TO GETTING ABSOLUTELY EVERYTHING
 YOU WANT by Mike Hernacki   0-425-10688-1/$4.50
A simple guide to the essentials in gaining wealth, success and
happiness in business or personal endeavors. This special ex-
panded edition has already enthralled America's top industries.

__PHONE POWER by George Walther   0-425-10485-0/$3.95
Your phone is your link to clients, business associates, merchants
and customers. Learn effective phone skills that will teach you
the art of using the phone as an information resource, how to get
in touch with virtually anyone, telephone "body talk", and the fine
art of Phonegotiating.

__FRIENDLY PERSUASION: HOW TO NEGOTIATE AND WIN
 by Bob Woolf   0-425-13039-8/$8.95 (Trade size)
Learn the most successful way to negotiate from America's
leading sports and entertainment lawyer. Negotiate efficiently
without making enemies. By the man named one of the 100
most powerful and influential attorneys in America by the National
Law Journal.

__THE 10 COMMANDMENTS OF BUSINESS AND HOW TO BREAK
 THEM by Bill Fromm 0-425-13039-8/$8.95 (Trade size)
 Identify the ten basic theories of business and learn how to
break them. The author provides creative, unique alternatives to
the conventional approaches used in business—alternatives that
prove you can have fun at work, increase employee morale,
and boost profits at the same time.

For Visa, MasterCard and American Express orders ($10 minimum) call: 1-800-631-8571

**FOR MAIL ORDERS: CHECK BOOK(S). FILL
OUT COUPON. SEND TO:**

BERKLEY PUBLISHING GROUP
390 Murray Hill Pkwy., Dept. B
East Rutherford, NJ 07073

NAME_____

ADDRESS_____

CITY_____

STATE_____ZIP_____

PLEASE ALLOW 6 WEEKS FOR DELIVERY.
PRICES ARE SUBJECT TO CHANGE WITHOUT NOTICE.

POSTAGE AND HANDLING:
$1.50 for one book, 50¢ for each ad-
ditional. Do not exceed $4.50.

BOOK TOTAL $ _____

POSTAGE & HANDLING $ _____

APPLICABLE SALES TAX $ _____
(CA, NJ, NY, PA)

TOTAL AMOUNT DUE $ _____

PAYABLE IN US FUNDS.
(No cash orders accepted.)